Lauren Resnick

Morgan James Publishing • NEW YORK

ISBN: 978-1-60037-838-6

Library of Congress Number: 2010936656

Published by:
Morgan James Publishing
1225 Franklin Ave Ste 32
Garden City, NY 11530-1693
Toll Free 800-485-4943
www.MorganJamesPublishing.com

Cover/Interior Design by:
Rachel Lopez
rachel@r2cdesign.com

Cover Illustration by:
Kat Chadwick

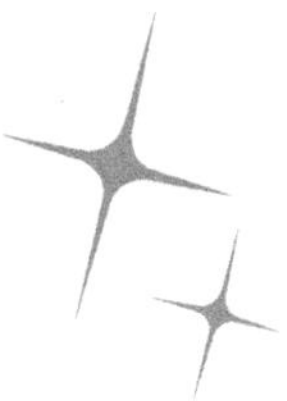

The idea for this book came to me while I was waiting for a flight for twelve hours at a tiny airport in Paris. It was my last stop before heading home to Australia, and in-between my second and third Diet Coke, the thought struck me that perhaps other girls could benefit from my travel experience, mistakes and chutzpa.

I do admit that I am a princess, and there's nothing wrong with that. It just means we "princesses" demand a little more than most, and we see obstacles not as problems, but challenges we must overcome to get what we want out of life.

This book is a guide for the princess who desires to see the world and experience more than her comfortable home, friends and society. This book will give you the confidence to get the most out of your trip – it's the stuff that the Lonely Planet won't tell you.

Thurs 25th Nov 12:28am, Paris Airport

Been thinking of ~~starting~~ writing book titled "travel guide for fussy girls" or something along these lines – think its a good idea, but could just be deliriously tired.

Subject matters:

- Sleeping in airports
- Food
- Stealing
- Smoking/Coffee/Diet Coke
- (Not) Exercising
- Relax
- Hair/Makeup
- Asking for help/looking good
- Shopping & carrying b/pack

cute stick figure pictures

Think it could be cute like Kathrine Eimars attempt - shoes & men?

Add this idea to list – Geltato boxes – Book

← was definetly over tired... still am.. haven't slept in I don't know how long - just downed 1st coffee since this morning. v. proud.

Could book: a bed, shower, new clothes etc.

Gotta stop spending $ but need good book to read after coffee - now awake. Half a til checkin.

Hmmm.

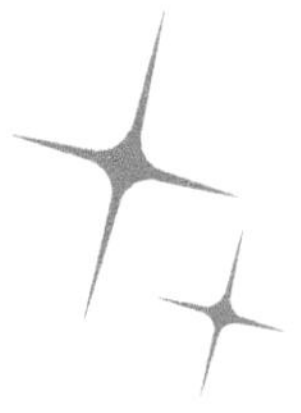

Acknowledgements

I would like to thank my family and friends for all their support and patience, especially with me harping on about this book. A special thanks to my Mum, Dad and sister, Simone. Sim - thanks for all your editing skills, being my travelling guinea pig, and, of course, for loving all things princessy.

Thanks to all my travelling girlfriends and their great advice; my cousin and talented graphic designer Becky; inspirational author Cyndi Kaplan; the boys at 2threads.com; Mimi Zu; Bessie Bardot; Tali Shine; beauty guru Denee Savoia and nutrionist Jackie Storm.

This book would not have been published if it wasn't for my mentor and friend Toney "Fitzy" Fitzgerald and, of course, the fantastic team at Morgan James Publishing, New York.

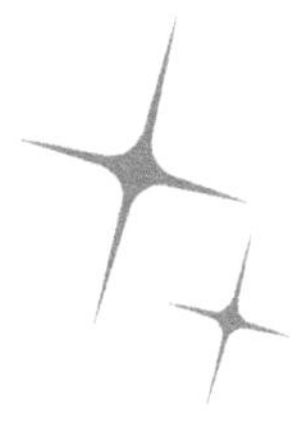

Table of Contents

day 2 or 3 – too many time z...

The plane ride from Shanghai to London was g-ross. We slept for sporadic periods – but unfortuneately woke up to eat – which was a total mistake. The food was so bad we couldn't eat it: thank g-d for the pack of almonds prepurchased in a Chinese supermarket prior to departure. I think I've eaten a total of 3 meals in 3 days – but have no idea ... I've lost count, ... really card...

中國東方航空
CHINA EASTERN
承运人 CARRIER CHINA EASTERN AIRLINES
航 班 FLIGHT MU551
日期 DATE 01 JUL
目的地 TO LONDON HEATHROW
姓 名 NAME RESNICK/LAURENMS
备 注 REMARKS
重要提示: 航班起飞前15分钟停止登机,
NOTICE: GATE WILL BE CLOSED 15 MIN...

possession. It must be surrendered on depa...
être presentée à la sortie d'Espagne. / ...

PLANNING AHEAD...

but not too much

"In retrospect, I would never walk in high heels during the day."

MIMI ZU, Fashion Designer

So many places, so little time…

Even if you already think you know where you want to go, do a little beforehand research. If you have enough money and no commitments, just explore and don't be afraid! Last-minute travel decisions are often the best and there will always be other travelers doing the same. Here are some hints for pre-travel planning:

Plan an Itinerary

When traveling for several months at a time, I recommend having a rough idea of where you want to go for about the first month. It also helped to have a couple friends with me during that time, so I could get used to being away from home and the European lifestyle. After the first month you'll be a pro!

I spent my first month in Greece and had pre-planned my accommodation for the first three weeks. I realized once I was there that all the pre-planning I had done was unnecessary and soon learned there will always be somewhere to stay, even at the last minute. In Greece, for example, there are people literally waiting for you to get off the ferry to offer you a room for a night or the week.

Read up on your destination before you get there. You don't want to miss out on something worth seeing. It will also make you really excited to get there and the hours spent travelling will all seem worth it. A good place to start is the *Lonely Planet* Travel Guides; you can also check out some of the websites listed in the *I Want More!* chapter at the back of this book.

I recommend travelling during the summer months in Europe – it's when everyone is out, you get the best tan and people are up for a fantastic time. It also means that you'll have to carry less in your pack (yes, I said carry), which makes travelling between destinations that much easier. It also, unfortunately, means that accommodations may be harder to find and more expensive, but it will be totally worth it.

At the Airport:

You will need to go through customs, where you will be required to fill in a customs declaration form. This includes details of where you'll be staying and for how long.

Remember to declare all items over a certain quantity or value, e.g. alcohol and cigarettes. Some purchases may require a duty tax.

How Long?

I travelled for around six months. I recommend splitting up one month between two countries and at least two days in one city, otherwise it's too rushed, especially if you have to travel for two to three days just to get there. Have a rough idea but remember that you can always alter your ticket if you change your mind. The length of stay will determine how and what you pack, who you meet up with and what places you want to explore.

Where?

I knew I wanted to be in Europe the entire time, so I picked a handful of "must-see" destinations and the rest was left to fate. Speak to as many people as possible beforehand as well as during your travels to learn about places you may not have considered visiting.

I chose places depending on climate, who and what type of people were going to be there, and events going on at the time. For example, do not arrive at a destination on a public holiday when everything is closed.

My plan before I left was quite different than the outcome of the trip. Before I left home my itinerary looked like this:

> Greek Islands – Italy – Spain – London – Paris – Amsterdam

It ended up looking like this:

> Greek Islands – Turkey – Croatia – Italy (including Sicily) – London – Spain – Portugal –Prague –Vienna – Salzburg – Munich – Paris

"... Have more fun. Last time I was too focused on our schedule."

BESSIE BARDOT, MODEL AND AUTHOR

YOUR TRAVELLING LIFE

Hostel Life

Nothing is more associated with European backpacking than staying in hostels. Similar to a YMCA, a European hostel provides you with a bathroom and a place to sleep. Depending on the hostel, you may have to share a room with others and you'll probably have to share a bathroom with many.

The first time I found out I had to share a bedroom with strangers, I panicked! I got used to it, and you can end up making really good friends this way – or even just someone to hang out with for the day.

You should definitely shell out around $25 to buy a Hostelling International Card (www.hihostels.com). If you plan to only visit big cities, there will be plenty of independent hostels and you won't need it. However, if you decide to go off the beaten track, many smaller cities and towns only have one hostel (usually one that requires you to have an HI card). If you happen to go to a town that only allows HI members, don't stress. You can often buy one there, or you can pay a fee and get a temporary membership for the length of your stay.

You can also consider purchasing a Hostels of Europe card for $16, which includes great deals with more than 250 independent hostels (http://www.isecard.com).

The Europe card is another service which provides discounts on rail and bus travel, travel insurance and discount flights. Do your homework prior to departure and you can save a lot.

It's important to take time out of traveling. Settle in one place for a couple of weeks and then set off again. Travelling can be exhausting!

So much to think about

Other considerations prior to travelling include money, passport, insurance and how you're going to manage squeezing in 12 pairs of Manolos into one teeny-tiny backpack.

Don't panic... I have it covered... just read on...

International Student Identity Card

Now that you've committed yourself to European travel, the next step is to stop by travel agencies that cater to students, for example, STA travel. These people know their stuff.

When you get there, you should first buy an International Student Identity Card (ISIC). An ISIC gets you tons of discounts and offers you plenty of services. While you must be a student to get an ISIC card, there is a $15 card available to anyone under 26 that offers similar (but reduced) benefits. Some of the services an ISIC card can get you include:

- Travel discounts
- General student discounts anywhere they are offered throughout Europe
- An email address
- Voicemail
- Phone card service
- Plane tickets

Now that you've got your card, it's time to purchase your plane ticket! This is where the student travel agencies really help out, as they can sell you flexible return tickets at much lower rates than are offered conventionally. This means you can change your return flight date for as little as $25 if you give proper advanced warning (as opposed to the standard hundreds of dollars) and you can also return home from a different city than you flew into. The cheapest places to fly in and out of are London, Zurich, Frankfurt and Amsterdam. For more info about flying around the world at really cheap fares, check out www.soyouwanna.com.

Alternatively, *Student Flights* will match ticket prices. Check out a few options before settling on one and you can save more money.

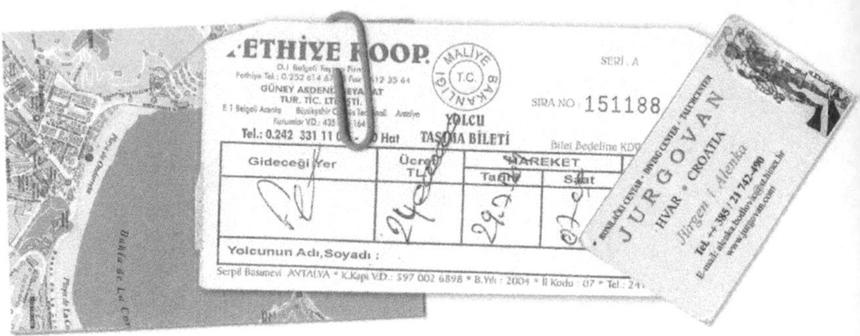

Passport

If you don't have one yet:

- Gather some proof of your citizenship (e.g., a birth certificate)
- Go to your local copy store and get two passport photographs taken
- Got to any post office or state/federal courthouse to apply for your passport
- Pay the passport fee
- The passport will be good for 10 years

Money

- TRAVELER'S CHECKS: These are great because if you lose them, you and your bank will have a record of the amount lost and they can be replaced.
- CASH: Easy to exchange, but if it gets stolen or lost you will not see it again.
- CREDIT CARDS: My friend took two credit cards; she placed one in a secret compartment in her backpack and

another in a separate money belt, which she carried at all times. That way if she lost one or a bag was stolen, she would not be stranded without backup. Good thinking!

Travel Insurance

So important! I managed to lose anything and everything of value on my trip. My wallet, mobile phone and camera were all stolen – luckily not my passport. Travel insurance was my savior! I could claim back what I had lost on the mobile phone stolen in Greece and the camera and purse stolen in Italy.

My insurance agency was QBE Travel Insurance, but shop around if necessary for the best deal. This one was recommended to me by my student travel authority. Spend the money – it's completely worth it.

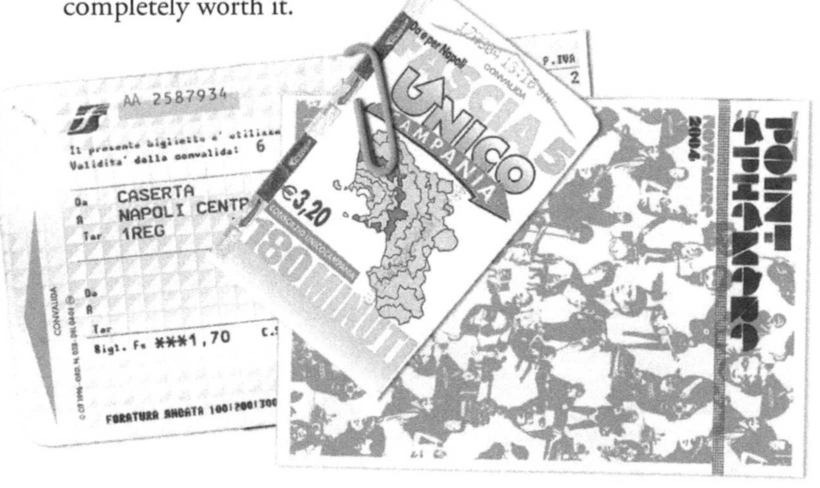

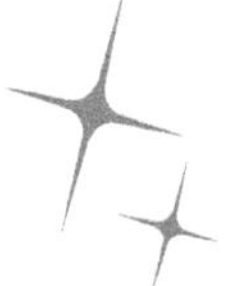

TOP 5 TRAVEL TIPS

From smartraveller.gov.au

1. **Check out latest travel advice**

   Go to smartraveller.gov.au for all the latest news about your next destination and subscribe to receive emails whenever new advice is released. It's an easy way to know what's going on around the world.

2. **Never leave Home without travel insurance.**

   It that simple. Just get it!

3. **Register your details online.**

   When you're away, register your details online with your local embassy. That way if something goes wrong or you're not contactable for a few days, you can at least know that someone has a clue where you've gone.

4. **Fine out if you need an entry visa.**

   Don't risk getting turned away at the airport! Check the entry requirements for countries, such as Turkey, where a visa may be necessary.

5. **Make copies of all your documents.**

   My mum always told me to do this and as annoying as she seemed at the time, she was right. Photocopy your visa, passport, credit cards, traveler's checks, etc. Take one copy with you and keep it in a safe place and give one copy to family or friends back home.

"My most difficult flight, by far, was flying from Cairo to Mykonos. We had just come back from horseback riding through the desert, snorkeling and climbing for four hours up a mountain in the middle of the night, not to mention, a 16-hour bus trip squished in with smelly men with roaming eyes, all with no sleep and while fighting food poisoning.

We were exhausted by the time we finally arrived at the airport, yet could not fall asleep. Maybe it had to do with the constant nausea, the rock hard airport chairs, or our bulky backpacks unsuccessfully serving as pillows. This was all in the name of saving a few bucks on flight prices. We finally fell asleep when the time arrived to board our flight. No one was around.

As our flight wasn't on the screen when we first arrived, we asked the information desk where to wait for our flight, and they directed us to a certain gate. To our dismay, they announced a change of our gate while we were sleeping."

SAFIE, 25

- pins
- shoes
- jeans
- c.d
- wax
- call flight centre 0061 0730117830

* Le Montclair Montmartre
62 Rue Ramey 75018 Paris
€20 - €23

* About square Caulaincourt
* Paris

JOSH
* 9365 5652

C

leather braclet

*

25th NOV.
* 3HOURS PRIOR

*

HEY, BIG SPENDER

Okay… you've stopped going to the hairdresser every weekend (only every second weekend) to save a little for the trip. How much will a six-month trip cost you? I would recommend around AUD $15,000. This, of course, depends on where you go and how much you shop, but that's a rough figure.

So take this as a guide no matter how long you intend to travel.

What will $15K get me? The latest Fendi clutch? Or this once in a lifetime experience? There is plenty of time for bags when you get back.

It will mean, however, taking trains and buses, sleeping in hostels and doing a lot of walking – but I wouldn't have it any other way. It's the only way to experience life in another country to the fullest.

MONEY TIP:

> You will get a better exchange rate in the country you are visiting, but ensure you arrive with the right currency and enough of it. You will need some cash, even if it's just to buy a bottle of water or pay for a cab.

Princesses have spent a lifetime on missions for the best clothes, shoes and handbags. It's not going to be easy walking past the birthplace of Prada and resisting a purchase.

The airport is cruel enough with all the duty-free items and the shops are practically begging you to buy while waiting for a plane. So what if you do? That pair of Gucci sunglasses in Rome's Leonardo Da Vinci and London's Heathrow airport blew your budget for the month, right?

This is your get-out-jail-free card girls. Here are a couple of ways to avoid paying as much as possible once you have started your travels.

Food:

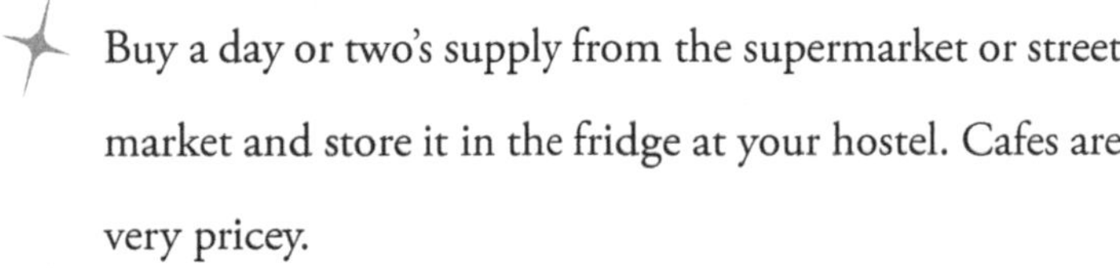

- Buy a day or two's supply from the supermarket or street market and store it in the fridge at your hostel. Cafes are very pricey.
- Find hostels that include breakfast in the cost of accommodation.
- Find work in a restaurant, café or hostel – desperate times call for desperate measures. This will allow you to earn money and get free meals. It will give you a chance to really live in a city and become fluent in an exotic language.
- Skip buying water at cafes and restaurants. You will save three Euros by purchasing bottles at a nearby supermarket.
- See more tips under Accommodations.

Alcohol:

- This one isn't too hard. You could score a free drink in Mykonos if you get up on the bar and dance! Don't expect it everywhere but it's worth asking in Mykonos, which is very unique! Let the bartender know you'll dance on the bar for a shot and in no time you'll be up there with a drink in your hand.
- Flirt with a guy. Don't be timid, but don't expect him to do this out of the kindness of his heart. A lot of guys will have ulterior motives so be careful who you ask.
- Buy a bottle of your favorite spirit and mixer and have a couple of drinks before you head out. Drinks at bars are ridiculously pricey (although, if you have a cute smile, you rarely have to buy your own drinks)

MONEY TIP:

Notify your credit card company you'll be away and not to worry if there's been a small purchase from Prada in Milan.

Accommodations:

- Give the manager those puppy dog eyes you've mastered so well, and then sweetly ask for a discounted price.
- Stay a week or longer (or say that you will) so they drop the price for a longer stay.

- Work at the hostel. It doesn't mean you have to clean toilets, but it may involve setting out breakfast or answering phones. Just something simple, and presto! You'll have more money for clothes, shoes, etc.

"To prevent running out of money, completely avoid taxis!"

CHELSIE, 20

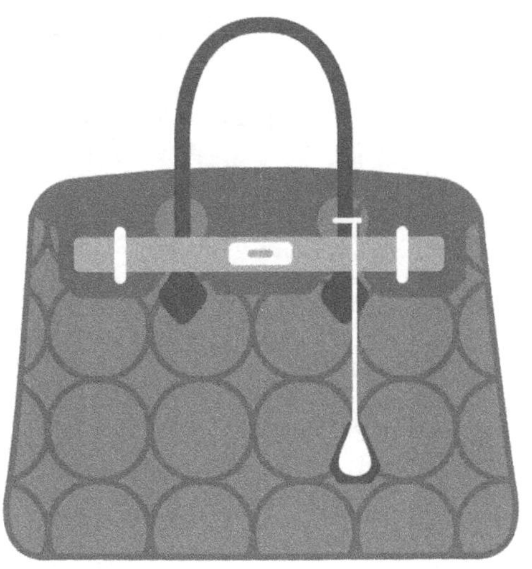

⟹ YQSTDG Ryan Air 10th Sept

5th sept / 12th sept. 00

Prag → Flight Czech Airlines CSA 220104626

or └ Prag - London $93 Easyjet

Italy 5 - 12th Sept

+ Milan - London (STN) 33€ 12th Sept
Ryan Air

+ Genoa - Milan - London • La Spezia ↓

+ Venice - Prag - London Thurs Night/ Fri Morn Milan 10am ↓
$40 $ $93

7th - 8th - 12/13th London 11am

Venice - Prague: 8th €120
(3 stops) 1237 -

+ LA SPEZIA → train MILANO : €17.97
↓ flight
LONDON : €19 + tax 13€
= €33

Friday 10.08.04
Flight FR4193
10:05am Dept Milano Bergamo (BGY)
11:05am Arrive London Stansted (STN)

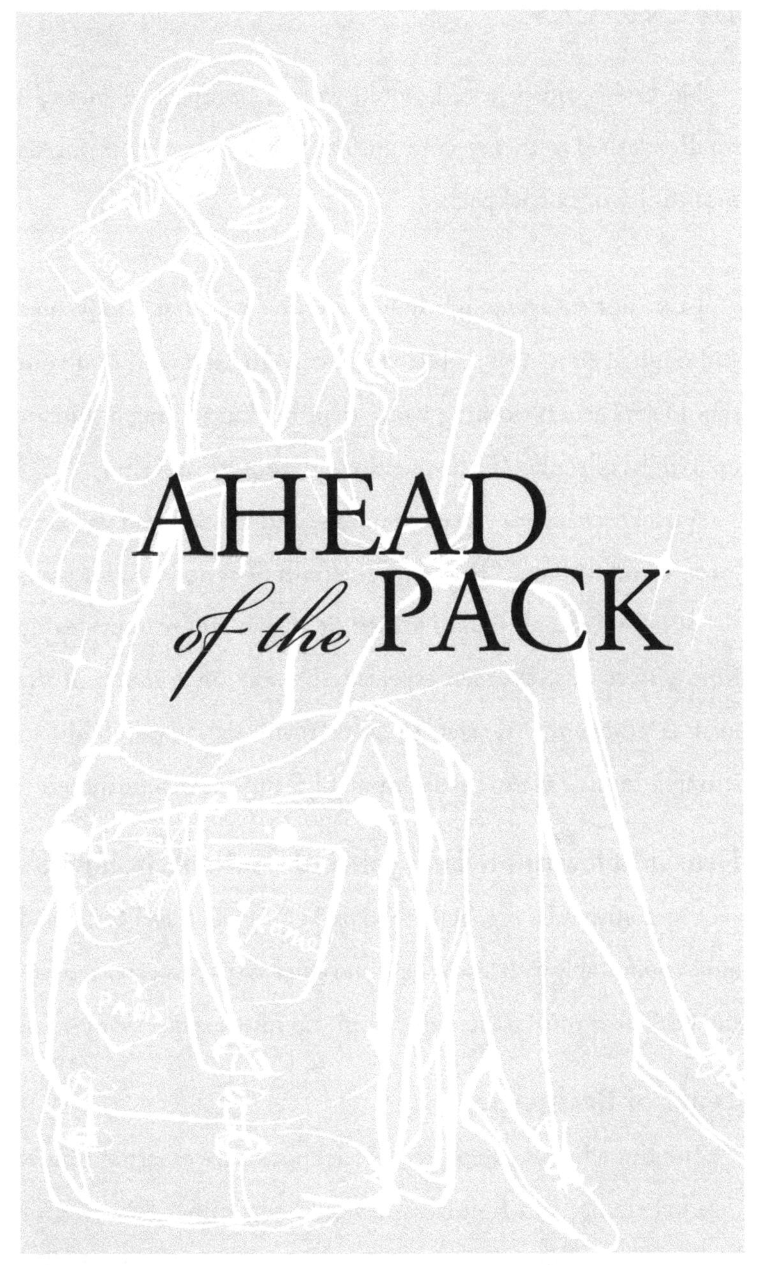

AHEAD *of the* PACK

Backpacks

No one could believe I would wear a backpack. I mean, it totally clashed with my cute outfits, but I did it. Yup, for six months I wore a backpack.

I can not stress enough how grateful I was that I took one. Although at times it feels like you're carrying the world on your shoulders, there is nothing worse than having to drag a suitcase up a flight of stairs. This is the ultimate tool for traveling.

A backpack allows you to be mobile and quick – you will even learn to run with one. Trust me: The train does not wait for you.

Well-packed and lightly loaded, it allows you to move easily from city to city. Women especially benefit since much of the load is efficiently transferred away from the upper body to stronger hips. (*Finally,* those "womanly" hips have a purpose!)

Here are a few tips to help you find a suitable backpack:

You don't need a big, bulky backpack. You will travel better and more comfortably with less. A light and efficient pack means freedom and flexibility; you'll understand when you hit your first set of stairs.

Types of Backpacks

The three broad categories of backpacks are external frame, internal frame, and frameless. I would recommend buying or borrowing an internal frame pack, as it is (relatively) not bulky, and provide easy access to your belongings so you don't have to rummage through your entire bag.

Internal Frame Backpacks

This is the type I used and I found it to be excellent – your clothes can be packed like in a suitcase and can organize all your belongings with ease. The brand I bought was called "Ambassador" by DMH Australia.

This pack had a smaller backpack attached to the front of the main pack, which I would unzip and use as a day pack. It also helped me balance out the weight when standing with the big pack on my back and small pack on my front. I looked like a bag lady, but you get used to it, and it becomes second nature.

How Much to Spend?

WHICH IS BETTER FOR TRAVEL: a pack that presents itself as not too fancy and is probably filled with t-shirts and panties? Or one that screams "I've got a Fendi Spy bag and Prada sandals inside?"

Spend around $200 to $300 for a new pack and choose a color that is simple and plain (boring, I know), but it'll make you look like you have nothing worth stealing.

Proper Pre-flight Backpack Preparation

A few simple precautions will increase your chances of arriving in London or Bangkok with the backpack in one piece.

1. The preferred method is to have your pack small enough to carry on. Airlines generally allow one carry-on article with total dimensions (height + length + width) 115 centimeters. A 50-liter pack will just meet these requirements. You may be able to get by with a little more.
2. If your pack is too large to be classified as carry-on, remove, tuck away or tie-up all straps, belts and appendages. Do not leave anything dangling that might catch in mechanisms.
3. Lock, tie-up or conceal all zippers on your pack so prying hands can't make a quick snatch.

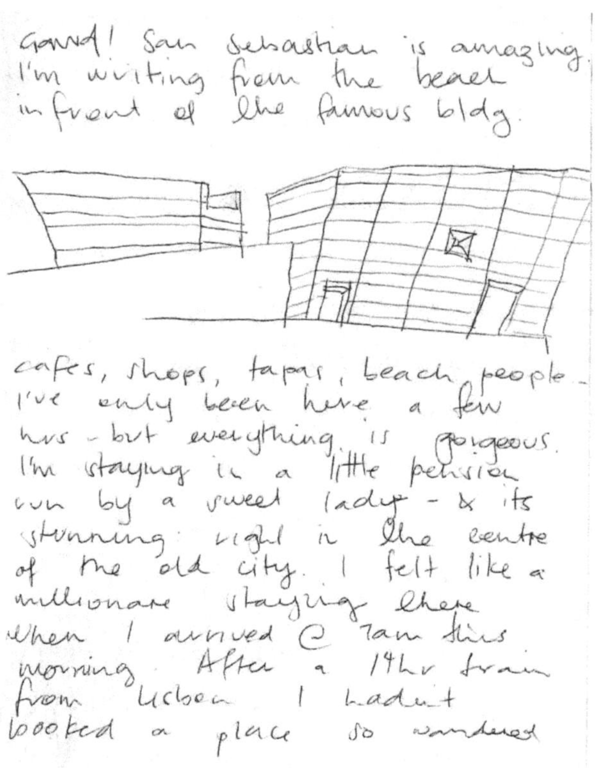
Gawd! San Sebastian is amazing. I'm writing from the beach in front of the famous bldg.

cafes, shops, tapas, beach, people - I've only been here a few hrs - but everything is gorgeous. I'm staying in a little pension run by a sweet lady - & its stunning: right in the centre of the old city. I felt like a millionare staying there when I arrived @ 7am this morning. After a 14hr train from Lisbon I hadn't booked a place so wandered

Sleeping Bags

Sleeping bags are great for keeping warm in airports and stations, on overnight trains and buses and for crashing on a new friend's floor. They're also useful for insulating yourself from "el-cheapo" hotel bedding. A good sleeping bag is more flexibile than any other item in the pack.

"You can endure great hardship as long as you can sleep warm."

SIR FRANCIS GALTON, *THE ART OF TRAVEL*, 1867

I first whipped out the sleeping bag when I traveled from Greece to Turkey. My friend and I caught an overnight ferry, but didn't realize that although we paid for our ticket, it did not guarantee us a seat. So the floor it was. We opened up our sleeping bags and they became our mattress while we snuggled up with scarves as blankets. Lots of other people were doing the same and we even met a bunch of young Greek travelers and ended up having one big sleepover party. It's all part of the experience!

Although you probably won't be camping on this trip, please take my advice on this… get a good sleeping bag and attach it to the outside of your pack.

There is no perfect sleeping bag for all seasons, conditions or uses. Every bag involves trade-offs among weight, stuff-size, comfort, warmth, weather resistance, durability and cost. Make sure you have one that is small when in its bag but also really warm.

For travel, the two sleeping bag designs to consider are those which are the most weight and stuff-size efficient: THE MUMMY and THE SEMI-RECTANGULAR

- The mummy is the most efficient in retaining body heat, since it incorporates a hood which, when fully battened down, leaves only a small circle of your face exposed to the cold. On warmer nights the hood need not be used.
- The roomier semi-rectangular lacks a hood but has a drawstring closure which can be cinched over your shoulders. A mummy will do this also. Some semi-rectangular bags have zippers extending across the foot section allowing the bag to open into a comforter, which is a very useful feature. A semi-rectangular will weigh a little more than a mummy for a given temperature rating, and substantial headgear will also be required to stay warm at that rating.

Choosing the Right Size

The roominess of a bag depends upon size and its dimensions across your chest, hips and feet. A spacious bag will not be as warm as a slightly tighter one, since the bigger bag has more inside air for the body to heat. If it's too tight, however, colds spots are formed where the insulation is compressed. You will also be less comfortable putting on additional layers of clothing should the conditions become extreme for the bag's temperature rating.

Sleeping bag models usually come in two or three sizes. The only way to properly size a bag is to get in four or five different ones. Outdoor shops allow and expect this. For me, roominess across the shoulders is a paramount consideration since I don't like feeling too constricted.

Sleeping Bag Materials

Inner shells are usually made of fine nylon or polyester, although some bags have a cotton/polyester inner liner. Cotton/polyester has less of a sticky or clammy feel against bare skin at warmer temperatures, but holds water and increases weight slightly. Most good bags have nylon or polyester inner liners.

Nylon is the standard outer shell. It is light, strong and the most breathable. No regular nylon, however, is better than mediocre for wind and water resistance. Rip stop nylon is stronger, more tear resistant and also more wind and water resistant. Polyester is more resistant to degradation from UV radiation than nylon and usually comes in micro-fiber formulations, which are more wind and water resistant.

How Much to Spend

Don't go too cheap with this one. It's important, warm and small. Discuss options with a camping store, but expect to pay around $200.

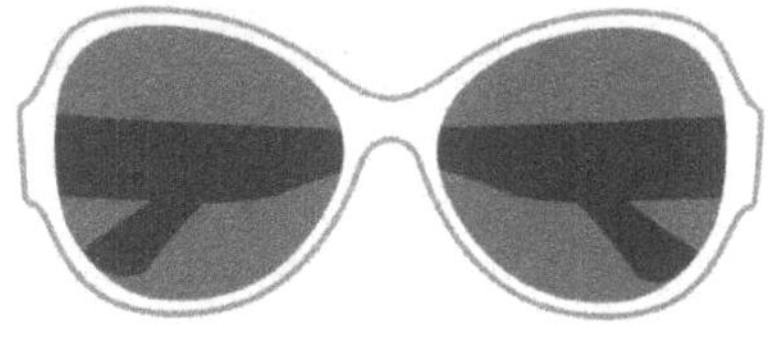

Care and Maintenance

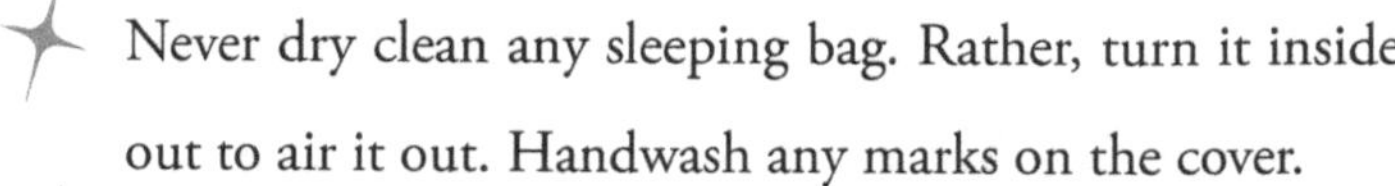

- Never dry clean any sleeping bag. Rather, turn it inside out to air it out. Handwash any marks on the cover.

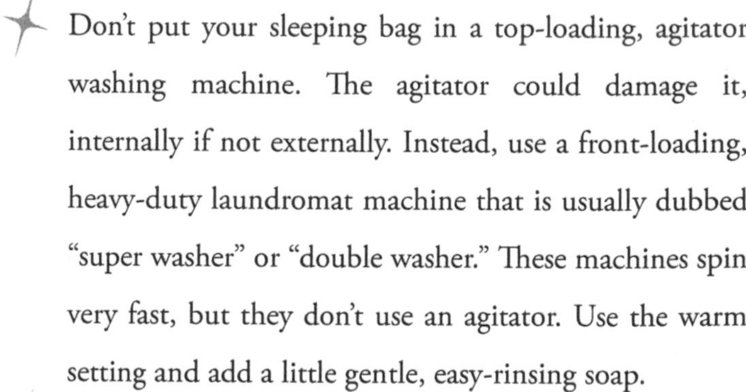

- Don't put your sleeping bag in a top-loading, agitator washing machine. The agitator could damage it, internally if not externally. Instead, use a front-loading, heavy-duty laundromat machine that is usually dubbed "super washer" or "double washer." These machines spin very fast, but they don't use an agitator. Use the warm setting and add a little gentle, easy-rinsing soap.
- To dry, set the dryer temperature on low or medium and throw it in. High temperatures could be harmful.
- Don't over wash your sleeping bag. Try spot washing for soiled areas. I only needed to wash my bag after several months of use. It sounds gross, but it will be fine if you can regularly air the bag out.

Don't store a sleeping bag in its stuff sack longer than necessary. This squashes the loft of any bag. Soon after reaching a campsite, hostel or hotel, I removed my bag and fluffed it with a few shakes. At home, I store it in a large cotton bag, which is supplied with most good bags.

Milano.

Caught the train from C.T. up to Milan w/ this German guy I met the night before @ mamas. So we spent half a day on the train & arrived in Milan just after siesta - perfecto timing. hit the shops.

I was blown away by the beautiful ppl, shops & class of this place - totally amazing.

Favourite furniture shop: CARTELL! amazing: phillipe Stark etc.. made me want to be a furniture buyer & travel b/w Syd & Milano buying furniture ~~fo~~ to bring back to Aust.

I HAVE *nothing* TO WEAR!

Packing: Key Items

(How to manage without 12 shades of denim… "you mean I can't pack it all?")

Before deciding what to wear, remember a few key points:

* You are taking a *backpack.*
* You will pack for *one* season.
* If you need or forgot something, *buy it there.*
* When you buy overseas, you don't need to fit it into you pack, there is always the option of sending it home via express mail and it will be there for your arrival!
* Packing ***light*** is essential for a backpacking trip.

Bringing even an eighth of your wardrobe is definitely out. It sounds impossible, but KISS (keep it simple stupid) is key here!! Try to take only the bare essentials. Most guides will tell you not to pack your sexy little black dress, your cotton candy pink cashmere sweater set or your four-inch high-heeled shoes, but I would have to disagree! As long as you can mix-and-match you'll be fine, but remember that you will have to wear things more than once – just be creative.

For example, when I went on what I thought was going to be a two-day trip to Amalfi coast, I packed a small day pack and brought the following: one light scarf, one t-shirt, one cute black pair of shorts, one bikini and a towel. I ended up staying four days. My scarf became a mini skirt, boob-tube, wrap and sarong… Think laterally – it's what we're good at!

Keep in mind that you will need to get maximum wear out of each garment you pack. Any article of clothing that you can only wear once or twice should be left at home. Key words to remember when selecting what to pack are: practical and versatile, cute and sexy!

If you simply *have* to have a blow dryer (save space by buying a travel-sized one) or curling iron (travel size butane ones are available), keep in mind that you will need power outlet adapters for all the countries you plan to visit. But remember, sea water takes care of straight hair woes and guys love a soft curl or crazy wave. It's the perfect time to test out a new style.

If you have long hair, bring along a small separate towel just for your hair. I bought a super-absorbent turban hair towel, made just for this purpose, available at K-Mart.

Finally… what you've been waiting to read: how to fit twelve pairs of jeans into a teeny tiny backpack? C'mon – I'm good, but not a miracle worker! Two pairs of jeans and that's it! I'm going to have to draw the line on this one. Here's a list of what else you'll need to bring.

SUMMER	PACKED IT!
Casual Shorts x2	
Sexy day/night shorts x1	
Skirt x 1	
Bikini x 2	
Small beach towel/mat – alternatively you could buy a cheap one there and then throw it away when you leave	
LBD* (please tell me you know what this is) *Little Black Dress	
Skin-color heels x1	
Jeans: Dark x1/Light x1	
Sandals x1	
Underwear x8	
Socks x3	
Bras x3	
Singlets x 4	
T-shirts x 3	
Summer dresses x 3	
Comfortable travel pants (cargo or loose pants) x1	
Light-weight pajamas x1	
Sneakers x 1	

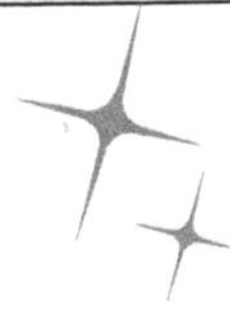

HOT WEATHER CLOTHING – remember these essentials:

- Insect repellent: you really don't want any nasty bites on your new tan
- Cool, loose clothing: very sexy and chic, while aiding in keeping you cool, like a kaftan
- Cute brimmed hats or a cap: make sure you love it because you'll need to wear it

WINTER	PACKED IT!
Waterproof puffy or woolen jacket/coat x1	
Jeans: Dark x1/Light x1	
Small towel x1 (although most hostels will provide you with one)	
Lace-trim thermal top x2	
Hoodie sweatshirt x1	
Boots x1– Make sure you can walk in them during the day or dress them up at night	
Sneakers/comfortable walking shoes x1	
Long-sleeve top x 3	
Warm pajamas x1	
Comfortable travel pants (cargo or loose pants) x1	
Thick socks x 3	
Beanie Hat x1	
Wool gloves x1	

Underwear x8	
Bras x3	
Black stockings/leggings/tights x1	
LBD x 1 (can be worn with black stockings for cold nights out)	

COLD WEATHER CLOTHING – remember these essentials:

- I recommend that if you are in Europe during the summer and move to a colder area, buy a coat there. It may take away from your budget, but unless you can convince your parents to send over your jacket/coat from home, it's not worth the hassle in summer when your bag is already heavy enough!
- Woolen thermal top: I got one that had a bit of lace around the neck line so I could double it as a top to wear for going out.
- A pair of track suit pants or gym pants: something comfy for those long bus rides or as a break from your daily jeans
- Woolen gloves, scarf and cute beanie
- Socks: very warm ones

MISCELLANEOUS ITEMS	PACKED IT!
PASSPORT	
Student ID	
Princess with a Backpack and *Lonely Planet* books	
Travel Insurance/phone numbers and info	
Traveler's Checks/money/credit cards	

Sleeping/Eye mask	
Toothbrush	
Shaver/razor/Nair	
Hair comb	
Soap	
Tampons	
Condoms	
Body wash/soap	
Moisturizer: body/face	
Shampoo/conditioner	
Makeup: Only the essentials —See Picture Perfect Chapter	
Tweezer	
Nail file	
Earplugs	
Tinted Face Moisteriser with SPF 15 (I love Dove or Pond's brand)	
Sunglasses	
Journal and pen	
Day & Night bag	
Camera + ipod + mobile phone (with all international charges)	

Additional Packing tips

1. Go Nude.

   Well, not literally, but think nude underwear. It works well under most pieces. Lace and mesh fabrics are good too as they can be scrunched up.

2. Roll it.

   For easy, wrinkle-free storage, tightly roll your cotton t-shirts, singlets and shorts.

3. Handle with care

   Pack your more precious items. Anything delicate should be packed in its own separate plastic storage bag to reduce damage.

4. Protect your clothes.

   Wrap high heels (if you can't resist packing them) in tissue paper so they don't catch on or dirty your clothes.

Just because you're going backpacking doesn't mean you can't look gorgeous. A little preparation and some smart packing will have you looking like you escaped to a spa retreat (well, at least for the first hour).

Organization and Packing______

(So you can fit in the important things, plus all the new shopping you're going to be doing...)

"The best way to pack is to be ruthless. You should be able to mix and match your whole suitcase, and don't forget to include layered options for colder climates.

Include sneakers along with some sassy dresses or top and pant matches for nights out. If an item can't be worn more than two ways, leave it at home. I like to roll all my items to avoid creases."

BESSIE BARDOT, MODEL AND AUTHOR

PACKING YOUR BACKPACK

All that into a backpack!?

It's important to be organized when you pack so you are able to fit as much in as possible (or necessary). Here are a couple really handy tips to help you pack all the items mentioned on the above list...and a little more.

Internal frame pack design requires semi-careful packing because the bottom of the load becomes part of the load-bearing structure. This is most apparent in packs with a bottom sleeping bag compartment.

- Put your shoes in the separate compartment at the bottom of the pack.
- Place your sleeping bag on the outside of your pack either at the bottom or at the top, depending on where your pack's straps for attaching the sleeping bag are located.

For the rest of the main body of the pack, place heavier items at the back wall of the pack, as close to your center of gravity as possible.

Your pack may have one or more access zippers, including one for the sleeping bag compartment, the top pocket and perhaps a panel to the main compartment. It's easy to place frequently needed items such as a camera and toiletry bag in strategic locations near these zippers.

Allow 10 percent empty space. This makes accessing the pack easier and life on the road better. And as you acquire new things, don't be hesitant about giving away or mailing back what you don't need.

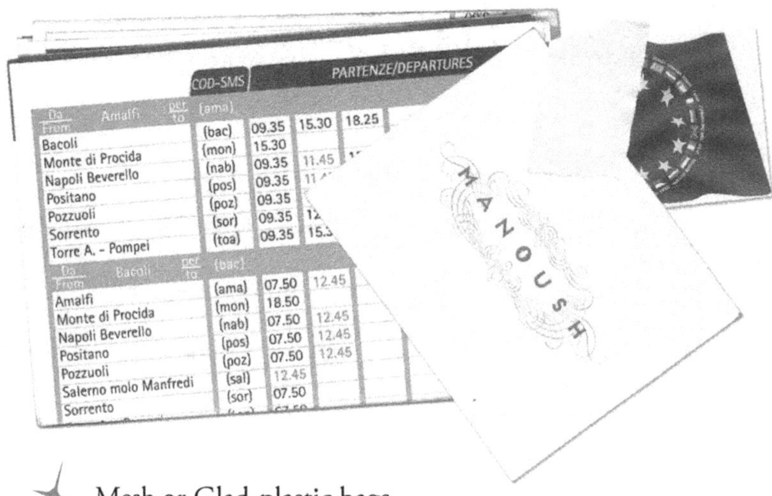

- Mesh or Glad-plastic bags

These are available from supermarkets for washing lingerie for about $2. The best ones, available from a

travel company called *Korjo,* are plastic and are super-durable. These can also be your chest of drawers, keeping like or related items together. Since you can see inside, locating and removing contents is faster. Put socks in the sock bag, tops in another, food items in the food bag, etc. Having several colors and sizes is helpful. It keeps everything neat and accessible. This is the best thing you can take with you and it will make living out of a suitcase so much easier.

Toolbag—aka: plastic zip freezer bags

I always have several in use. Freezer bags are thicker and last longer. Premium brands with sliders reseal easily. These are great for items like shampoo bottles to avoid leaks.

The tool bag is a nylon, mesh or plastic zip bag which contains items I don't need often, but are necessary to have. It's kind of like a first aid kit.

This bag should include occasionally needed items, such as detergent, matches, spare razor cartridges, earplugs, Panadol, rubber bands, etc.

Personal Kit

I used a mesh or plastic zip freezer bag to contain the items I use the most: toothbrush, toothpaste, hair pick, razor, soap/shampoo, a small bottle of roll-on deodorant, a pair of folding scissors and a small mirror.

Travel Laundry

Unfortunately you will have to do some laundry yourself. I know, where do you start? You've never done this before, but neither had I.

Here are a few tips:

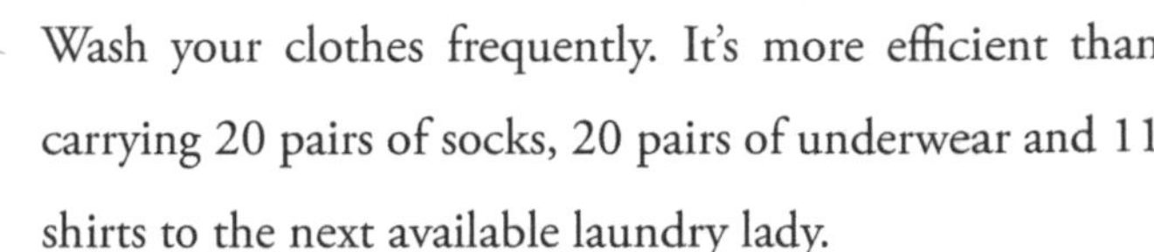

- Wash your clothes frequently. It's more efficient than carrying 20 pairs of socks, 20 pairs of underwear and 11 shirts to the next available laundry lady.
- Note that the "90" setting on international laundry machines represents 90°C, which is nearly boiling. Not knowing this, I shrunk a favorite jacket half-a-size and transformed the rest of my clothing to shades of gray.
- Buy a small box of washing detergent from the local store and transfer the powder into a small zip-lock bag.

Hand-washing socks and other tricks

- Place your hands inside the socks and scrub.
- A good way to hang clothes without clothespins is to double-up the cord and twist it together a few times, then tuck your clothes between the two cords.
- If you are going to be washing clothes in sinks (which you will), bring along a flat rubber drain stopper that fits

over drain holes. You can buy one at your supermarket for $1. Otherwise use your least favorite sock, which saves weight, space, and a buck!

It sounds simple enough... but don't pack anything that requires dry cleaning only!

Istanbul.

T.C. Kültür ve Turizm Bakanlığı

Ministry of Culture and Tourism

AYASOFYA MÜZESİ / *HAGIA SOFIA MUSEUM*

- BU BİLET YALNIZCA AYASOFYA MÜZESİ İÇİN GEÇERLİDİR.
  THIS TICKET IS VALID ONLY IN HAGIA SOFIA MUSEUM.
- AYAKLI KAMERA VE FOTOĞRAF MAKİNASI İLE PROFESYONEL ÇEKİM YAPMAK ÜCRETE TABİDİR.
  PROFESSIONAL CAMERA RECORDING IS SUBJECT TO A FEE.
- SATILAN BİLETLER GERİ ALINMAZ.
  TICKETS ARE NON-REFUNDABLE.
- BİLETİNİZİ GEZİ SÜRESİNCE SAKLAYINIZ.
  PLEASE KEEP YOUR TICKET DURING THE VISIT.
- BU BİLET YALNIZCA BİR KİŞİ VE BİR SEFER İÇİN GEÇERLİDİR.
  THIS TICKET IS VALID ONLY FOR ONE PERSON AND ONLY FOR ONE TIME.

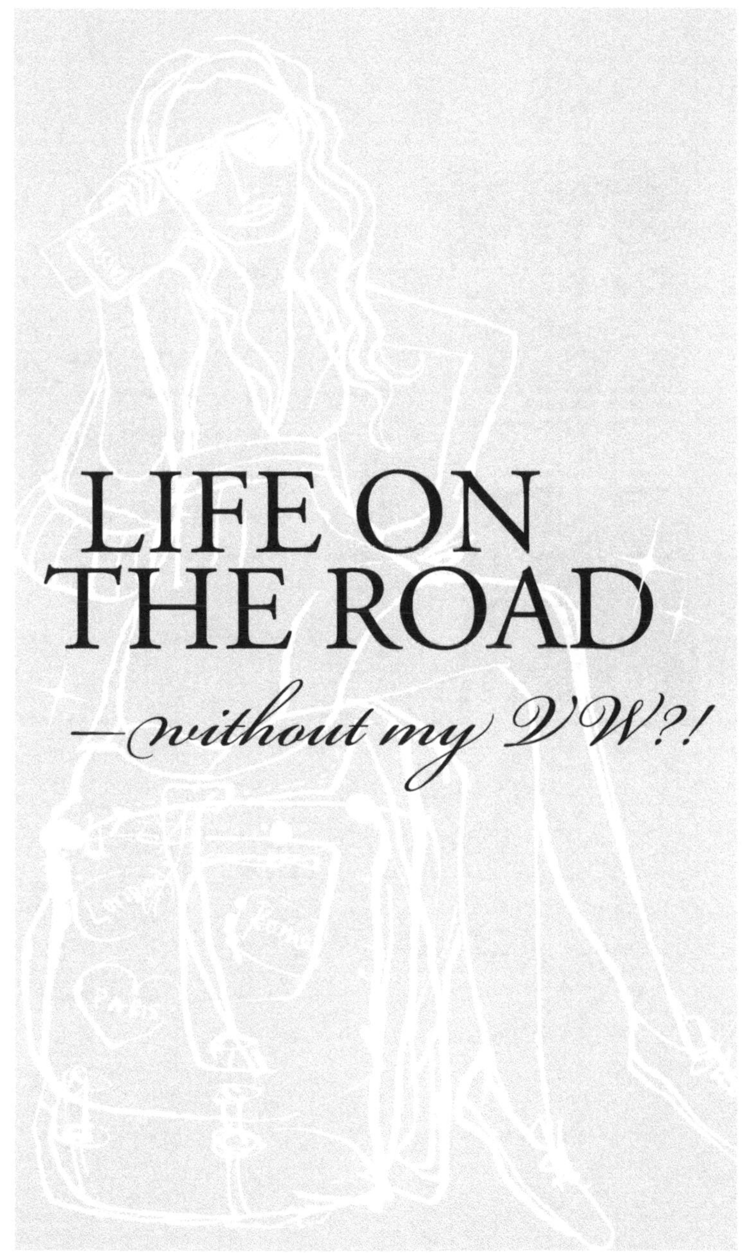

LIFE ON THE ROAD

—without my VW?!

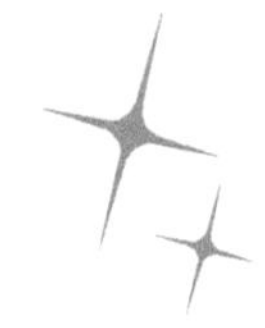

..nterior of the Hagia Sophia

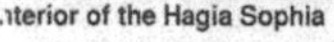

Spice seller in the Spice Bazaar

After a 14hr bus ride from Fethyer we arrived @ Istanbul metro bus station. It was noisy, crowed, with the worst toilets we've come across thus far.

We arrived w/out accomodation booked & so our first task was to find a place to stay for the next 3 nights.

We managed to find an avaliable room @ Sultans Hostel & so proceeded to get from the metro to Sultanmet - the buzzy part of Istanbul.

After almost getting on

Type of Travel

Trains, buses, taxis and good old-fashioned walking are what you'll do. All are types of travel we don't often rely on in our convenient world back home. These are where the real adventures happen and where you will meet weird and wonderful people. It will really make you appreciate the simplicity of home.

"Adventure is something you seek for pleasure, or even for profit, like a gold rush or invading a country. But experience is what really happens to you in the long run; the truth that finally overtakes you."

KATHRINE ANNE PORTER
American writer

Ways to Travel…

To Eurail or to not Eurail?

EURAILPASS

The Eurailpass allows unlimited rail travel through 17 European countries for a specific amount of time ranging from

15 days to three months. The countdown begins the day of your first train ride. If you are under 26, you get a break on the price, but it is still a reasonable deal without the discount. My only caution is the Eurailpass encourages some people to travel too much, too far and too fast. You may not want your most lasting European impression to be through a train window.

Take advantage of Europe's train system. To do this, you need to get a Eurail pass. These passes are by far the easiest way to get around. Getting a pass is so helpful that you should buy one before you leave home at your student travel agency.

I chose to pay as I went instead of getting either option, because I wasn't sure where I wanted to go and for how long I wanted to stay. If you are organized before you leave, the Eurail could save you a lot of time and money.

Basic Types of Passes

Eurail Global Pass

The Eurail Global basically allows unlimited travel in 18 Eurail Global countries.

Eurail Select Pass

With a Eurail Select Pass, you can design your own pass by selecting three, four or five bordering European countries.

Eurail Regional Pass

Perfect for travelers who want to see a small part of Europe in a shorter time frame! You can select from 20 Regional Passes. Options include:

- Austria - Croatia/Slovenia
- Austria - Czech Republic
- Austria - Germany
- Austria - Hungary
- Austria - Switzerland
- Benelux - France
- Benelux - Germany
- Croatia/Slovenia - Hungary
- Czech - Germany
- Denmark - Germany
- France - Germany
- France - Italy
- France - Spain
- France - Switzerland
- Germany - Poland
- Germany - Switzerland
- Greece - Italy
- Hungary - Romania
- Italy - Spain
- Portugal - Spain

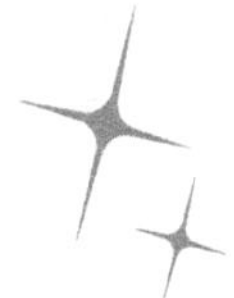

Eurail National Pass

There are 15 different National Passes available.

- Benelux
- Croatia
- Denmark
- Finland
- Greece
- Holland
- Hungary
- Ireland
- Italy
- Norway
- Poland
- Portugal
- Romania
- Spain
- Sweden

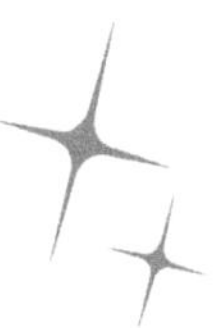

Eurail Pass covers 17 countries: Austria, Belgium, Denmark, Finland, France, Germany, Greece, Hungary, Italy, Luxembourg, Netherlands, Norway, Portugal, Republic of Ireland, Spain, Switzerland and Sweden. It can be bought for travel on consecutive days or scattered days. The consecutive days must be used on consecutive days. The price depends on your length of travel. To qualify as a youth, you must be under the age of 25.

	ADULT	YOUTH
15 Days	$554	$338
21 Days	$718	$499
1 Month	$890	$623
2 Months	$1,260	$882
3 Months	$1,558	$1,089

The Eurail Flexipass can be bought for use throughout any two-month period.

	ADULT	YOUTH
10 Days in 2 Months	$654	$458
15 Days in 2 Months	$862	$599

All prices are approximate at the time of publication. See website for up-to-date prices: http://www.eurail.com/

Other Info

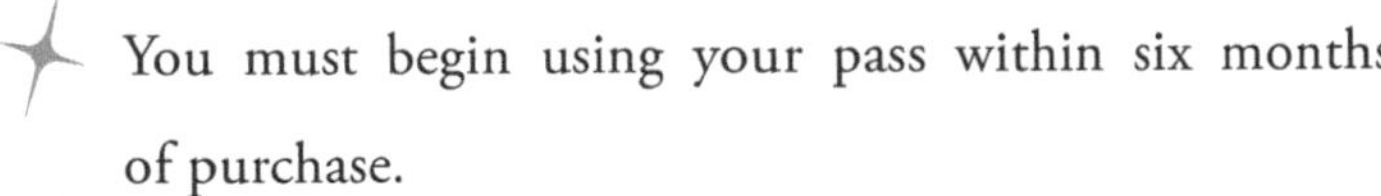

- You must begin using your pass within six months of purchase.
- You must mark each date of travel in the space provided on your pass BEFORE getting on the train. Usually this is not a problem, but some stuffy conductors—or those fishing for bribes—will give you a hard time otherwise. Though quite rare, the penalty you could face would be the cost of the train trip, a $100 fine AND the confiscation of your Eurailpass. It's not worth the risk. Just remember to fill out your pass before boarding.

- Any day of travel actually begins the previous night at 8 p.m. This is a huge perk of which you should take advantage. Travel by night train as often as possible since you'll want to be seeing cities during the day. Plus, it saves you one night's accommodations. Of course, if you've got enough cash, you can still save the day for sightseeing and buy a bed in a sleeper or couchette on a train, usually for about $20.
- While the passes entitle you to free travel on any train in the given countries, sometimes you still have to pay a reservation fee for a seat. This is true of most specialty or high-speed trains, and certain countries always or often require it, such as Spain and Italy. But don't worry, even with the reservation fee, you're still saving crazy amounts of money.
- The pass offers group discounts, even for groups of two.

If you want to save even more money, you can buy a Euroline pass, good for unlimited bus travel between selected cities for 30 or 60 days. The travel time is much longer and your options are much more limited (many countries only have one city included), but the price is nice. It ranges from $249 for a youth traveling 30 days in the off-season to $449 for an adult traveling 60 days in the high season. There are bathrooms on board, so you can do a quick touch-up before hitting your next destination!

Just remember Eurail may not be the best option for you and could end up costing you more than buying an individual ticket each time you want to travel. Speak with your travel agent or customer service representative to find the plan that's right for you.

BUSABOUT

See Europe your own way with Busabout Explorer. Basically, it's a hop-on, hop-off network and they have designed it for people like us - independent travellers who want choices as they travel with every opportunity to change their mind as their trip develops. It's a great feeling rocking up to a city and deciding to stay a week instead of just a night. Busabout Explorer gives you the flexibility to do exactly that.

See as much as you can on a whirlwind trip or relax and take your time. You can get value Loops and Flexi Trips are valid all season so there's no rush.

Another option is to have your trip organized for you. Try the "Busabout Adventure" to do that.

Busabout Adventures showcase some of Europe's popular destinations, including sailing around the stunning islands of Croatia, exploring Italy's incredible history or even discovering the wonders of Egypt.

These great value trips are an awesome way to see the world, especially if you are unsure of what you want to do when. It may help give some structure to your trip and is a great way to meet new people. By travelling with experienced guides, you'll immerse yourself in local living, take in the sights and chill out with plenty of time to explore.

For more information and special deals, visit www.busabout.com.

BUSES/COACHES

The best way to find out about which buses go where is to call or visit the main bus depot in the city to which you are going. They will generally be cheaper than trains but often take a lot longer. Buses may be the only option sometimes as trains may be booked out and don't always stop at specific destinations.

They are also reasonably comfortable and make stops every two hours. This allows you to move around, stretch your legs, grab a cup of coffee and prepare for the next two out of a 12-hour stretch.

It's a great way to see parts of the country that wouldn't be possible on a plane.

Check out http://www.setra.de, which is just one of many companies available in Europe to help you get to your destination in comfort.

WALKING

With comfortable shoes, a light pack and a new city to explore, this is matchless pleasure. Stop at a cool café in Paris for a hot chocolate, try on shoes in Rome or watch a street performance in Barcelona. The choice is yours and you have all the time in the world to enjoy it.

Walking tip:

> Pack super-comfy walking shoes or sneakers. Blisters are no fun – and a seriously bad look.

Whatever you want to do, you can do. Now that's good traveling.

Now, all this travel on the road will require you to crash in unexpected places. Travelling is tiring, and you will want to sleep at any given opportunity. Expect to find yourself sleeping in the airport lounge, train stations or even beaches. At least it saves you a night's worth of accommodation costs. Read on for a few tips to make sure you are safe and possibly even get some sleep!

"You must do the thing you think you can not do."

ELEANOR ROOSEVELT, AMERICAN STATESWOMAN

It was by now the 20th August & I had planned to meet Jane & Ed in Rome. So I got a sardine like overnight train to Rome & @ 8:30am walked to Casa Olmata hostel by myself again & loving it. Was v. exciting to get to Rome - felt like the beginning of a new phase of travelling - big cities. No more beaches! Was v. anxious about this fact, by it was Rome - I cant complain.
So I get to the hostel & meet this Israeli guy & we decided to walk round the city for the day (as he was leaving that night) & we had a picnic by the river - looked @ sites & shops & headed back for me to unpack later that day.
The hostel was really cool & very social. There was a roof top packed w benches & tables, a t.v

BEAUTY SLEEP

"Sleeping" in airports

You may find yourself having to stay overnight in many different, weird and wonderful places. Not all of them will be comfortable and most won't.

I use the term "sleeping" loosely as it *can* be done (especially when you're tired and hungry), but often doesn't happen.

Sleeping in airports is the No. 1 free place to sleep. Here is what you'll need to get you through this challenge.

 Essentials:

- Sleeping bag: use as mattress
- Four seats: use as bed
- Day pack: your new pillow
- Pashmina (cashmere/wool): your blanket and best friend

 Music:

- iPod: play sleepy chillout music or sad love songs (warning: do not play if missing family/friends or if PMSing).

 Read:

- This book
- Inspirational and romantic travel books, e.g., *Almost French* or *The Bride Stripped Bare*
- Start a journal
- Newspapers: So many events happen while you are away from home. It's good to read the news every

once in a while, otherwise you never know what's going on otherwise.

- Trashy magazines: as many as possible – they bring you back to reality

Food:

- Try to stop at a supermarket before you get to the airport. It's much cheaper and you can stock up on the following: nuts, Diet Coke, tuna, bread, cheese/dips/peanut butter, fruit and water.
- Don't skip this food advice – if there are no shops open at 2a.m. you'll be so grateful for those snacks.

"Athens airport is open 24hours. Not so scary. Make sure you have your sleeping bag out and find a girl or group to spend the night with."

SAMANTHA, 20

Warnings:

- Watch your luggage! If you're in a sketchy place, sleep on your backpack as well as your day pack.
- Don't fall asleep with your cleavage showing. It just causes trouble. Put 'em away for another time (trust me, they come in handy).

- Keep all money, credit cards etc. under your shirt or even in your bra. At least you'll definitely feel that disappear!

"Three items I can't leave home without are Chanel red lipstick, creed millesimé fragrance, mac lip balm."

MIMI ZU, FASHION DESIGNER

OVERNIGHT TRAINS AND BUSES ____

The number two semi-free place to stay is overnight trains or buses. Some Eurailers plan every evening for another city six or eight hours away. The advantages are obvious. You save on a room and you get to your destination early enough to have a big day, find accommodation or locate a shady park for extra snooze time. You may meet other backpackers doing the same and team up with them for accommodation the next night.

When you take an overnight bus, avoid headlight glare by choosing the side away from oncoming traffic. The front of the bus is the most frightening, the middle of the bus has the smoothest ride, and the back of the bus is the roughest, noisiest and smelliest, although the very last row sometimes affords a luxurious multi-seat stretch-out.

For both trains and buses, place your pack under your feet or otherwise secure it. Your big bag goes in storage underneath the bus, small bag should be between your feet or on your lap. Just remember: your passport and money should be under your clothes.

This isn't always fun, and you may have to put up with people around you snoring, talking loudly or talking to you when all you want is a good night's sleep! These are just some of the painful times of traveling, but just think – when you arrive at your destination, a whole new world and culture awaits you. It's worth it!

"Always pack earplugs! Someone will always be snoring. Sleep is so precious – losing it is not an option."

NICOLE, 27

Stations

Train stations are the number three free place to stay. In many larger European train stations (but not all), there is a nightly ritual of travelers bedding down for a few hours. Just see where others are crashing, select a safe looking bunch and crash beside them. Ask if they mind starting a conversation. Everyone sees safety in numbers, so perhaps with a pretty smile or luck, you won't be too dangerous looking.

First, though, you may want to check your pack in luggage storage or a locker. Just take out your sleeping bag, mesh clothes bag for a pillow and pad, if you have one. If you can't or don't want to check your pack, you may want to tie it to something next to you and/or to yourself. Otherwise, use it as a pillow, or at least keep it between you and a wall. You don't want your pack to look like an easy mark and you'll sleep better.

Then relax and have a good sleep. I usually pop in foam earplugs. I've always been able to get at least a few hours of sleep, but once I slept for 10 hours straight. Travel can be tiring!

Station policies differ regarding freeloaders. Sometimes the police come around and ask to see onward tickets. Sometimes you can buy one and cash it in later. Sometimes they ask to see passports. Sometimes they ask you to take a seat. Sometimes they come around early in the morning and order everyone to get up and move on. Sometimes they tell you to move on, and then *they* move on.

Always nod your head and agree, and be as respectful as possible. They are just doing their jobs. Whatever the station policy, you can rest assured that it is no big deal, that it is handled in an orderly and civil manner as long as you don't cause trouble and that they don't have any interest in you other than not seeing you.

Beaches

Number four for a snooze is on the beach, which is fairly common among some backpackers in Mexico, Greece and the south of Spain, among other places. Guidebooks such as *Let's*

Go and *Lonely Planet* even list areas where beach crashing is common and where it is dangerous.

Don't sleep alone though, and try to find another group to crash with.

Public City Parks

Number five sleep-free place is in public parks. Don't do it. I've heard too many stories of people having their packs stolen or worse, the clothes on their backs stolen! If you find yourself pressured by others to do this, remember this advice.

Hostels

Although you may have to crash at some smelly station, train carriage or bus overnight, the majority of your sleeps will be in hostels.

Look for women-friendly hotels. Some hotels now have special rooms designed with the female traveller in mind. The rooms may even be in a safer location, not down a long hallway or facing a deserted car park.

These are not five-star hotels, so be prepared to lower your expectations of accommodations. But remember, you'll barely be in here; so the uglier the room, the more adventurous you can be! I have listed just a select few places, but for more cities and hostels, go to hostelworld.com.

The places I stayed are listed below. However, make sure you do some research either on the internet or your *Lonely Planet* guide, and choose a place you feel comfortable with. There are new hostels popping up all the time. I often find the best place to stay is based on a recommendation from fellow travelers.

GREECE	
MYKONOS	**Hotel Vencia:** Rohari, Mykonos Town, Mykonos, Cyclades, 84600 This was pricey (around 62 Euros a night), but it was peak season. It included breakfast and had a pool, bar and unbelievable view. This was our most extravagant accommodation.
IOS	**Marcos Beach Hotel:** Mylopotas, Cyclades, Ios Island 84001 More of hotel than hostel, but nothing flash. Has a pool (with sun lounges – essential, of course!). Free b/fast if you wake up in time – highly unlikely in this party town.
SANTORINI	**King Thiras Hotel:** Fantastic staff, breakfast, rooms and views! Not right in the center of town, but the value is great.

TURKEY	
FETHIYE	**Ferah Hostel:** 2.Karagözler, Ordu.Cad.Nr:21, T – 48300, Fethiye Quaint, friendly, great b/fast, big dinners – great communal feel.
ISTANBUL	**Sultan's Hostel:** Akbiyik Cad No:21, Sultanhmet/Istanbul Good area, clean, nice staff. Great b/fast omelets and big coffees.
CROATIA	
DUBROVNIK	Try to find some friends to share an apartment. The best place to start is to go to the local tourism office in the city centre. They will organize viewings of rooms and apartments available.
HVAR (ISLAND)	As above
ITALY	
AMALFI	**Scalinatella Hostel:** Piazza Umberto I, 5-6 | Amalfi, Campania, Italy, Amalfi 84010, Italy Just 10 minutes walk from the center of Almalfi… rooms aren't great, but you won't be spending time in them anyway.
CINQUE TERRA	Anywhere in Riomaggiore – it's the best of the five villages, heaps of young, single people, so don't worry that it's gorgeously romantic as well. The accommodation is advertised on the streets, just pop into any of the accommodation offices and inquire about a bed/room.
ROME	**Casa Olmata:** Via dell'Olmata 36, Rome, 00184, Italy. You can walk there from the train station which is good. Friendly staff and heaps of Aussie travelers. They also have 1 Euro pasta nights – eat as much as you can fit in.

ROME *(cont'd)*	**The Yellow Hostel:** Via Palestro, 44 00185 - Rome (Italy) Rome's classiest and sexiest accommodation. It's new and trendy – not typical of a normal hostel.
FLORENCE	**Paola Fazzinni:** Borgo Pinti 31 50121 Firenze, Italy This is a b&b exclusively for women. It's minutes away from the Uffizzi Gallery and the main train station.
SICILY	
TAORMINA	**Taormina's Odyssey:** Trav. A di Via G. Martino, Italy. I loved this one. It's small and quaint, lots of Aussies and great Italian coffee with b/fast.
CATANIA	**Agora:** Piazza Currò, 6, 95121 Catania, Sicily, Italia The rooms were very average, but I met fantastic people here, and there's a huge bar, where young people flow out onto the street.
CEFALU	I managed to find a group of people who were staying in the same hostel in Catania to take me along with them to Cefalu, and we stayed in a run-down apartment. It did, however, have more Sicilian charm than we could have hoped for – a must. I loved it. Try **Casanova B&B:** Via Porpora 3. Charming, with all the extras.
SPAIN	
BARCELONA	**Gothic Point:** c/vigatans, 5 08003 Barcelona. I liked the community feel, free breakfast, and activities such as Gaudi tours and Spanish lessons available and run by hostel staff. Smile nicely to the grumpy front man to get a good bed.

BARCELONA *(cont'd)*	**Centric Point Hostel:** C/ Passeig de Gràcia, 33 Five minutes from Las Ramblas, this hostel is modern, spacious and light-filled rooms on one of Barcelona's most famous avenues.
GRANADA	**Oasis:** Â Placeta Correo Viejo, 3 Loved this place! It was really easy to make friends here. The atmosphere was chilled and had a community feel to it. Great kitchen and nice rooms. Don't get here at night by yourself though, it's tricky to find.
SAN SEBASTIAN	**Adore Plaza:** Constitucion Square 6. Great hostel – clean, great bathrooms, perfect location. Try to pre-book as they are popular in the summer months. If you want to treat yourself, go exploring – there are heaps of gorgeous pensions that are more $, (where you'll get your own room and bathroom) but you will feel like a Spanish princess.
PORTUGAL	
LAGOS	**Rising Cock:** Travessa do Forno 14, Friendly and fun. Has a kitchen and you even get dinner cooked for you! They are famous for their booze cruises.
AUSTRIA	
VIENNA	**Wombat:** Grangasse 6, 1150 Vienna Pretty nice for a hostel. Bar is safe and central location.
CZECH REPUBLIC	
PRAGUE	**Clown and Bard:** Borivojova 102, Prague 3, Zizkov Not a favorite, but has a good bar downstairs – a great place to meet heaps of people (especially in winter).

PRAGUE *(cont'd)*	**Czech Inn:** Francouzska 76 , 101 00 Praha Czech Republic This is the only designer hostel in Prague. The cafe and bar are great places to meet fellow stylish travelers over a local Czech beer.
GERMANY	
MUNICH	**Wombat:** Wombat's City Hostel Senefelderstrasse 1 Munich Nicer than in Vienna – it feels like a hotel. Has a café/restaurant/bar.
BERLIN	**Circus Hotel:** Weinbergsweg 1a 10119 Berlin. Gorgeous and modern. This hostel comes highly recommended. You can grab a bed in a dorm or private room.
FRANCE	
PARIS	**Hotel des Jeunes (MIJE):** 6, rue de Fourcy, 75004, Paris. Gorgeous, safe and central location. This one is expensive, but worth it! Watch out for the large school groups. Ask for a small (3-4 person) room. **St. Christopher's Inn:** 159, rue de Crimée, Paris Opened in 2008, this is the newest Backpackers Hostel in Paris and there is even a female-only floor – the Oasis. Here you can escape the boys, enjoy a few extra creature comforts and hit the Streets of Paris – with space and style.

"You're bound to have the person next to you turn and chit-chat. Start hanging out with them. Hostels mean that you meet other travellers, which means you get comfortable

hanging out with them, which means you don't make the effort to meet local people, which means you don't get to experience the real life in the city. Making only one local friend means you will be invited out and shown the best places to eat, shop and go out. Having met a friend in Portugal, I was shown their favorite restaurant; tried the best local cuisine and got to hang out at their local pub. No tourists were to be found at any of these places and I got a real taste of what the country is about. Staying in a local residency I also got to experience everyday life. Do as the locals do and avoid tourist attractions as much as possible. This is difficult in summer season when locals all on holiday and tourists are mainly around."

KAREN, 25

After settling showering we went for lunch & exploring the city. Surprisingly, the city was really green & the hippodrome, blue mosque & Anya Sophia - all tourist attract's where surrounded by parks & neatly shaped gardens, & just around the corner from us as well.

After eating we decided it was time for some RNR & deep clean scrubbing. We walked up the road to one of the highly recommened Turkish bathes, paid $25 for bath & massage.

The interior was magical

Interior Dome.

water trickles down ~~from~~ marble through gold taps onto gnd.

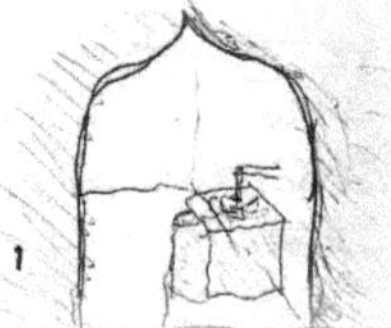

This old turkish woman scrubbed me down with an exfoliator then covered me in soap & massaged my weary travelling muscles for 20mins. After that Sim & I lay in the centre of the bathe on a huge marble circular bench for a steaming & relaxation. It was the most luxuriant thing we've done for ourselves since we began travelling.

After feeling soft & clean we went back to our room & had a nap followed by dinner on the roof & an early night.

PICTURE PERFECT

You want to look good at all times, but you're stuck in a tiny bathroom, with one unusable plug and fluro lighting! Here's what to do:

 Hair:

* Sea water is amazing for curls, just make sure you leave it to dry after being in the ocean. Don't touch or it'll go frizzy.
* Make sure you take the right products and not too many. Just a good smoothing serum for after the shower should help tame your mane.
* Body hair is tricky. Definitely wax before you go and try to find places along the way, but the next best thing is Nair (if you're untalented with a razor like me).
* Prepare: apply a deep conditioning treatment before you leave – it will give your hair fantastic shine.
* Texture: if you have wavy hair, don't waste time blow-drying it straight. Comb a light cream conditioner through damp hair and tie in a low pony for a really sleek and sexy look.
* Keep it chic: Hair tends to go frizzy in humid conditions. Comb a silicon serum through your hair before landing. Try John Frieda Hair Serum.
* Protect: You will be out in the elements most of the day, be it in the sun or snow, so look after your

locks. Try a UV protector, such as KMS Perfection UV Protector.

"Always carry wax that comes prepared on the strip. All that's required is to separate the strips, place and rip! Carry powder foundation or oil blotters as different water from different countries can make your face shiny. Plus, you don't want all those photos of you from Europe to be of you with a shiny face."

NICKY, 28

Soft, glowing skin – its easy!

The stress-free traveler will have a glow about her. All that sun, sea and excitement radiates from you when traveling. Who's kidding – we all need a little hand now and then. Try these tips:

- Use a tinted moisturizer instead of cover-up, foundation, powder, etc – they're just not necessary and moisturizer gives you a great natural glow. I used Pond's Tinted Moisturizer in "honey" color. It can be used both day and night, so take a couple. You don't want to run out of this stuff!
- Sea water again: It is fantastic for the odd spot, so make sure you get plenty of salt water, and drink as much natural water as you can fit in, ideally three liters a day.

- Glow: apply a self tanner the day before you get on the plane. I'm a huge fan of Johnson and Johnson's Holiday Skin Night; apply it before bed the night before you leave and you will wake up bronzed! It is too easy.
- Hydrate! Being on a plane really dehydrates your skin. Try a moisturizing cloth mask such as Biotherm's Source Therapie Tissue Masks. They come in slim individual packets and will rehydrate your skin in 10 minutes. Use one before you leave, and then again when you land.
- Remember to look after your eyes. An eye cream works wonders for tired, over-stressed eyes. A great budget eye cream, such as L'Oreal Visible Results eye cream, is all you need to take away those puffy bags.
- Super clean: get silky smooth with an exfoliator. Once you land and get into a shower, gently massage a little on your face and body, and follow up with a rich moisturizer.
- Sunscreen your skin: my friends know me as a sun worshipper, but it's far worse not being able to party all night because you're burned. It not only damages your skin, but also makes you really tired – and you will need all the energy you can get being a traveller. Try Nivea Sun Moisterising screen lotion SPF 30+. It's easy to apply and doesn't leave a chalky residue.

Make-Up to Go

Don't waste time piling makeup on your face. There's better ways to spend your days. Make sure you add this to your essential kit – and keep it simple!

1. Tidy your eyebrows.
2. Add a touch of concealer around your (hung-over) eyes.
3. Highlight your cheekbones with a bronzer/blush.
4. A good coat of mascara (waterproof, of course).

The following are a few excellent tips from Denee Savoia, a top beauty therapist from Sydney:

- Aveda Fillables are perfect for storing small quantities of your favorite products. If you are spending an extended period overseas, make sure you take enough of your fave products, especially if they're not available in remote locations.
- Don't bother packing mascara if you're heading anywhere tropical, unless it's waterproof. NEVER take pump packs – they'll end up all over your bag. I once packed my fave body moisteriser (pump pack) and, even though I wrapped it in a plastic bag, the stuff still ended up all over my clothes.
- If you're going to be spending loads of time in the water, take a leave-in conditioner.

- If you're doing a lot of air travel, take vitamin E or cod-liver oil tablets for your skin.
- Keep your hands soft on long haul flights by smothering them in vitamin E cream and popping a pair of clean socks over them while you're sleeping.

NOTE:

Looking good while traveling is something I could have learned the benefits of much earlier in my journey. You will be amazed at the difference in how people treat you when you have a backpack on, if you're wearing decent clothes and have done your hair. Even when you are in the most grubby situation (i.e., been on a bus for 14 hours) try to give your hair and makeup a touch-up when asking for directions or buying a ticket – it really makes a difference (especially in Europe).

"3 items I wouldn't leave home without...

1. My Tali compact and lip gloss
2. My Amex
3. My mobile"

TALI SHINE, AUTHOR AND MODEL

More hot beauty tips from my fellow female travellers:

1. Try Shu Uemura cleansing beauty oil – a make-up remover and cleanser extraordinaire – which is two very essential products in one. Especially when I travel, I like to make sure I wear sunscreen on my face and this product takes everything off easily and quickly. No blocked pores or oily residue = happy skin.
2. When travelling on a beach holiday, pack a few hot oil hair treatments to use on the road to help hold back the sun and salt damage.
3. After washing your hair, sleep with conditioner in hair while covered with a disposable shower cap. The next day your hair will be so soft and smell so nice.
4. Always carry a small bottle of perfume. It will make you feel good, so no matter what else you're wearing, you wear it with confidence.
5. Since flying dries the skin, carry a moisturizing mask to use the first night you get off the plane. Preferably, use a put-on and wipe-off mask so it's hassle free.

6. Always collect samples of products to use on trips so you don't have to carry lots of big bottles and jars.
7. A good lip gloss and eye liner is often all you need to look dressed.
8. Carry all wet items such as shampoo, conditioner, body wash, razor, toothpaste, etc, in doubled up ziplock bags. Then pack all of them in a cosmetic bag with plastic lining. This prevents spills onto your clothing.
9. Wear a smile all the time because it makes you feel good, look good and it's infectious.

To Avoid Jetlag:

1. Drink lots of water on the plane. Lay low on sugar, caffeine and salt because it'll make you look puffy.
2. Try to sleep on the plane. If you have two flights, stay awake on the short leg and try to sleep through the long leg.
3. Try to book your ticket so that you arrive during the day. Make sure you stay up until early that evening and have an early first night to get adjusted to your new time zone.
4. Adjust your watch/ipod/mobile to local time as soon as you arrive.

Packing the Perfect In-flight Bag

There are new rules in Australia for what kind of toiletries you can take on the plane with you. Remember to check with your own country's authorities prior to boarding. Your travel agent should be a useful source of information.

Make sure containers with creams, drinks, perfumes and gels do not exceed 100ml and are in a clear plastic bag. There is a limit of one bag per passenger. This will mean down-sizing your beauty essentials. Trial sizes are also a fantastic way of getting all you need on the plane with you.

ESSENTIALS:

1. Lip balm
2. Moisterizer stick
3. Handcream
4. Eyecream
5. Eyedrops
6. Skin refresher spray
7. Deodorant — roll-on
8. Nail file

I kept reminding myself was a completely surreal experience

Im now writing on the ferry which we boarded @ 7.30am & got kicked out of our seats 4 times until we decided to find out where we were actually meant to be sitting.
We've also managed to have another 2 coffees. May be I should start a tab...

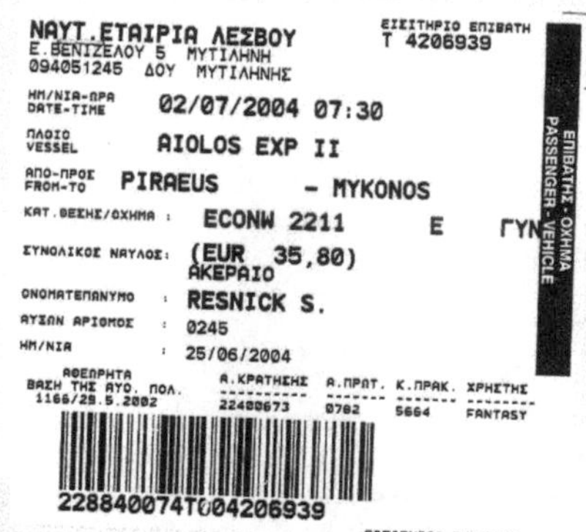

ΝΑΥΤ.ΕΤΑΙΡΙΑ ΛΕΣΒΟΥ
Ε.ΒΕΝΙΖΕΛΟΥ 5 ΜΥΤΙΛΗΝΗ
094051245 ΔΟΥ ΜΥΤΙΛΗΝΗΣ

ΕΙΣΙΤΗΡΙΟ ΕΠΙΒΑΤΗ
T 4206939

ΗΜ/ΝΙΑ-ΩΡΑ DATE-TIME 02/07/2004 07:30
ΠΛΟΙΟ VESSEL AIOLOS EXP II
ΑΠΟ-ΠΡΟΣ FROM-TO PIRAEUS - MYKONOS
ΚΑΤ.ΘΕΣΗΣ/ΟΧΗΜΑ : ECONW 2211 E ΓΥΝ
ΣΥΝΟΛΙΚΟΣ ΝΑΥΛΟΣ: (EUR 35,80) ΑΚΕΡΑΙΟ
ΟΝΟΜΑΤΕΠΩΝΥΜΟ : RESNICK S.
ΛΥΣΗΣ ΑΡΙΘΜΟΣ : 0245
ΗΜ/ΝΙΑ : 25/06/2004

ΑΘΕΩΡΗΤΑ ΒΑΣΗ ΤΗΣ ΑΥΟ. ΠΟΛ. 1166/28.5.2002

Α.ΚΡΑΤΗΣΗΣ	Α.ΠΡΑΤ.	Κ.ΠΡΑΚ.	ΧΡΗΣΤΗΣ
22480673	0782	5664	FANTASY

228840074T004206939

ΕΠΙΒΑΤΗΣ - ΟΧΗΜΑ
PASSENGER - VEHICLE

← Finally we decided to get food after 8 hrs of not eating. We thought we could hold out until mykonos (as there was only rubbish to buy) but I asked if they had anything else. thankgawd again – I didnt know if we were going to make it lack of sleep & food not a good combo Feel better

DOES MY BUM LOOK

big in this?

Now, my closest friends and family know how pedantic I am when it comes to being healthy, but even *I* wasn't concerned about calories while I was travelling. I do, however, believe eating well is the best way to prevent getting sick and stay in top form. I couldn't think of anything worse than being starved while trying to fit in all that I wanted to do every day while on the go.

Jackie Storm is a Nutrition and Health Educator who lives in New York. She has some great advice for keeping healthy while traveling. Check out some of her tips below or go to her website www.jackiestorm.com. Keep her advice in mind, but remember to always try a little of the local cuisine and enjoy!

Jackie's Tips

- Depending on how far you are from home, you may need a few days to adjust to the new time zone. You can help yourself adjust by sitting in the sun for about 20 minutes a day to reset your internal clock. Many travellers also swear by a melatonin supplement, which is taken shortly before bed.
- Keep your protein intake high during the day for optimum energy while travelling. Protein sources include fish, poultry, lean meat, eggs, cottage cheese and yogurt.
- Unwind at the end of the day and help yourself get a good night's sleep by saving some form of starch or

carbohydrate to have at the end of the day. Carbohydrates raise our serotonin level and help us fall asleep.

- ❑ Yogurt with active yeast cultures can be a good thing to eat on a daily basis while travelling. It can help protect you from bacterial infections.
- ❑ Drink lots of water, but you may want to make it bottled water. The water in other countries might be safe for natives, but may contain bacteria our G.I. system has not been exposed to.
- ❑ Save some bottled water to wash your fruit in. Alternatively, choose fruits with a peel that can be removed and thrown away.
- ❑ Choose cooked vegetables in preference to raw. Again, this is about avoiding exposure to bacteria that may be on raw vegetables.
- ❑ Avoid deep-fat fried foods.
- ❑ Stay conscious of portions and stop eating when you are no longer hungry.
- ❑ Travel with a ziplock bag of mixed nuts and dried fruit in case you get stranded without immediate access to food.
- ❑ If travelling to a tropical climate, keep in mind that your body will need slightly more salt than usual to compensate for the salt that will be lost in perspiration.
- ❑ Leave room in your meal planning for an occasional indulgence. Skip the potato, have the chocolate cake.

The following is Jackie's list of sensible snacks that can provide you with instant energy as you make your way through Europe. When travelling to some remote areas, you should pack a variety of non-perishable treats in your backpack before you leave. You never want to be stranded without food – trust me!

- English muffin, wholegrain toast, rice cakes & peanut butter
- Natural yogurt
- Cottage cheese
- Greek salad
- Small carton of milk
- 1 large apple, 1 pear, 1 small banana
- Chicken rice soup
- Italian salad with mozzarella cheese and tomato
- Minestrone soup
- 1 cup chicken noodle soup
- Walnut halves, almonds, brazil nuts, pistachios and air-popped popcorn
- Hard-boiled eggs
- Fruit salad
- Tuna and crackers

My favorite on the go foods were:

- Canned tuna (in Europe look out for tuna flavors such as Mexican, American, etc, which contain other ingredients such as capsicum and corn. It's tuna and salad in one!)

- Fruit and veggies – buy a small tub of cream cheese or hummus and dip
- Soy and skim milk box-drinks are known as long life; they can be stored without refrigeration before opening
- Nuts: all kinds – peanuts in their shell are fun to peel and help pass the time when bored (yes, sometimes even peanuts can entertain you)

These are great choices since you will often be without a fridge, and these foods have a long shelf life.

Just remember, you'll be walking all the time, so don't worry about your weight – just keeping healthy is enough!

"Do not travel to escape life, but travel so that life does not escape you."

AMERICAN WRITER

Mykonos

A place for beautiful people. In the day you go to the beach, sleep in, eat... but its nighttime where mykonos comes alive. At 12am the clubs/bars start to fill up – everyone is out; its an awesome atmosphere.

↖ Huge Club in Myk – gets started round 3am

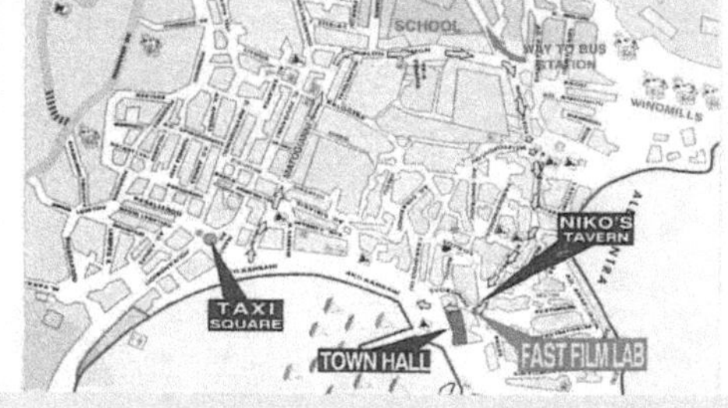

THE BEST LIST

starts with an A

Parties in Europe can rock your world. Here is a list of my favorite clubs and bars.

Party hard girls!

CITY	PARTY
MYKONOS, GREECE	**Space Nightclub**; Lakka square, Mykonos Town (starts at midnight). Like everywhere in Mykonos – hot people, great music. Book in advance if you want a private booth on the side of the dance floor. **Cava Paradiso**; Paradise Beach, Mykonos (starts at 4 a.m.)- watch the sunrise as you party on. **Tropicana Paradise Beach** (starts at 5 p.m.) — what better way to end a great day of tanning than to go for a boogie and cool drink while on the beach! **Bolero Bar**; Town Centre – very cool R&B on Thursday nights. **Full Moon Party** @ Paradise Beach…grab a bus if your accommodation is in the town centre.
IOS, GREECE	**Q Club;** Ios Main Road, 840 01 Ios, Cyclades – great R&B! Can't go wrong here. Cheesy music not your thing? Then skip this island… **Satisfaction** – Aussie-owned small bar, good vibe.
SANTORINI, GREECE	**Enigma; Fira 24024** – English/Greek mixed music, great atmosphere and hot interiors. **Murphy's; Fira 25291** – Big Aussie hangout, cheesy and young...but lots of fun

HVAR - CROATIA	**Carpe D'Em** – hottest people, incredible music, head over after a full day of tanning from 5-8 p.m.... You've been warned!
FLORENCE, ITALY	**Meccanò**, Viale degli Olmi 1, Florence, Italy 50100 (where you might meet a V.I.P. or two), and the fabulous **Andromeda**; Via dei Cimatori 13, Florence, Italy 50123 or cool bars such as **Tenax**; Via Pratese 46r Firenze, 50145 — very popular with locals; and **Flog**; Via Michele Mercati 24b **Firenze**, 50139, which is great to watch live gigs.
MILAN, ITALY	**Brera** is known as Milan's original hotspot; every bar here is fantastic. Glamour oozes from every door and this is a great area for an evening stroll. You can't pass the **Just Cavalli Café**; Via L.Camoens Milan, 20123 – supreme design and oozing style, the flamboyant fashion designer has created another masterpiece to enjoy (even if the shoe and handbag combination is out of your reach).
LAGOS, PORTUGAL	**Whyte's Bar**, and **Three Monkeys** are great places to meet people or get into some serious drinking, although, the whole town is a party.
SAN SEBASTIAN, SPAIN	Head straight to **La Parte Vieja**. The streets in the Old Town are packed with people from 11 p.m. (dinner) until 4 a.m.; this town is pumping, especially on weekends. **Illumbe** is where to head for after hours partying, with a dozen clubs staying open until 6 or 7 in the morning.

BARCELONA, SPAIN	Gothic Quarter and Olympic Port. Walk the gorgeous streets and discover the hundreds of traditional and chic bars available. Try **Milk;** Gignas 21, in the Gothic Quarter; **Buda Restaurant; c/Pau Claris 92/08010** - which is ideal for kicking off the evening, Buda gets glamorous on Tuesdays with Model Night; and **Rubi Supper Club and Lounge;** Banys Vells 6 bis, Barcelona 08003 - in the Borne/ Ribera District. The gorgeous restaurant turns into a bar at around 11:30 p.m. with Latin tunes and funky crowds. I fell in love with **Bestial**; C/Ramon Trias Fargas 2-4 Old City. Expensive, but luxurious and glamorous – come here for lounge music and great cocktails on a hot summer's night.
BILBAO, SPAIN	**K2**; Somera, 5 Bilbao, Vizcaya 48005; **La Granja**; Plaza Circular, 3 Bilbao, Vizcaya 48001; **Celtic's** and **el Consorcio** – great places to start the night and **Serantes**; Licenciado Poza, 16 Bilbao, Vizcaya 48011, among many others, is the get-together area for the young people of the city and sometimes the streets are positively overflowing with people.
LONDON, ENGLAND	The better-known clubs tend to be around the Leicester Square/Charing Cross Road area. For example, **The Mean Fiddler;** 157 Charing Cross Road, London WC2H 0EL, is a flamboyant-friendly, glammed-up favorite. Other clubs worth seeking out are **The End Club**; 18 West Central St Bloomsbury WC1A 1 JJ, **The Fridge;** Town Hall Parade Brixton London, SW2 1RJ, and famous **The Ministry of Sound; 103 Gaunt St London, SE1 6DP.**

LONDON, ENGLAND *(cont'd)*	For something a little more subdued yet glamorous, head to **Sketch**; 9 Conduit Street, London, W1S 2XG – a seriously sexy bar and restaurant; or the stylish **Kingly Club**; 4 Kingly Court, Soho.
PRAGUE, CZECH REPUBLIC	The area around Wenceslas Square is the hub of club entertainment: these are usually found down one of the many arcades e.g. the extremely popular **Duplex Dance Club & Café Bar**; Wenceslas Square 21, New Town, Prague 1. Don't go past **Karlovy Lazne Dance Club**; Novotneho Lavka 5, Old Town. This is for serious clubbers. Spread over five floors, this is the biggest club of its type in Central Europe. Or try **Radost FX;** Belehradska 120 Prague 2. Great atmosphere with a fun, young and affluent crowd.
VIENNA, AUSTRIA	The most popular area at night is the so-called "Bermuda Triangle" — the area around Ruprechtsplatz, Seitenstettengasse, Rabensteig and Salzgries. There you will find bars such as **First Floor**; 1 Seitenstettengasse Vienna which is so cool – it opens at 3 a.m. on Sunday! You can try something different like a live-music venue such as **Der Neue Engel**; Rabensteig 5 Vienna, 1010.

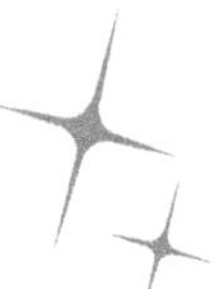

VIENNA, AUSTRIA *(cont'd)*	The club scene is spread out in Vienna; at places like **Volksgarten;** Burgring 1 Vienna, 1010 or **U4**; Schönbrunner Straße 222 Vienna, Vienna 1120, where there are heaps of young people and mainstream music – which is always fun. **Walk into Flex;** Donaukanal/Abgang Augartenbrücke Vienna, A-1010, which plays mainly independent music, hip hop, drum and bass, trip hop and all sorts of electronic tunes Viennese style, of course.
SALZBERG, AUSTRIA	**Bierklinik** and **the Hell;** Rudolfskai 26 Salzburg, 5020 at the Rudolfskai are a couple of good pubs. On the opposite side of the river Salzach, there is the **Bajazzo**; Giselakai 17a Salzburg 5020, which is cool with an outdoor area, which is great in warmer months.
MUNICH, GERMANY	Schwabing is Munich's entertainment center where small theatres, cabarets, cinemas, pubs and bars congregate in this area. Cool nightclubs to head to include **P1;** Prinzregentenstrasse Munich or the famous party hot-spot **Pacha;** München Gastronomie GmbH Maximiliansplatz, 5 80333. For a new sleek and sexy bar try **Ododo;** Buttermelchstrasse 6. Great interiors and hot bar staff. The former dumpling factory turned nightclub **Kultfabrik;** Grafingerstrasse 6 | ex Kunstpark Ost, Munich 81671, is next to Munich's Eastern railway station (Ostbahnhof) is a huge party hub.

PARIS, FRANCE	Cool bars like the **Hotel Coste**; 239 rue St-Honore, 75001; and **George V Hotel Bar;** 31 Avenue George V are both an amazing experience. **Café Charbon;** 109 Rue Oberkampf 75011, or **the Bar du Marché**, 75 rue de seine – 75006, which stay open until two in the morning. **The Queen;** 102 Au Des Champs Elysees 75008**,** and **The Bains;** 7 Rue du Bourg-l'Abbé 75003, are beacons in the Parisian night, but clubs such as the **Barfly**, 49-51 av George V, 8th M George V, **Le Cabaret;** 2 Place du Palais Royal 75001, and **Barrio Latino;** 46-48 Rue du Faubourg Saint-Antoine 75011, are also very cool. Don't forget to catch the famous (art of the nude) shows at the **Moulin Rouge;** 82 Boulevard de Clichy Montmarte 75018, and **Crazy Horse;** 12 Avenue George V 75008.

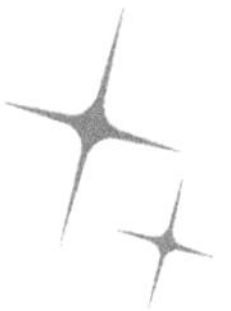

Monday.

Time for the Grand Bazaar - finally. 4500 shops, 1 day, 2 girls. We set off early & for 6 hours we did not stop. It was a fixed building, but had a market-like quality to it. Goods such as glass lamps, jewels, traditional guitars, bags, clothes etc were all available. It was a great experience - really felt like turkish markets hundreds of yrs ago (but done up a bit). We even stopped for a turkish lunch @ a no-name corner stand where we ate chicken, tomato & onions on stools in the middle of the male "stock market" - all these guys on mobile phones presumably finding out prices of gold to inform the local

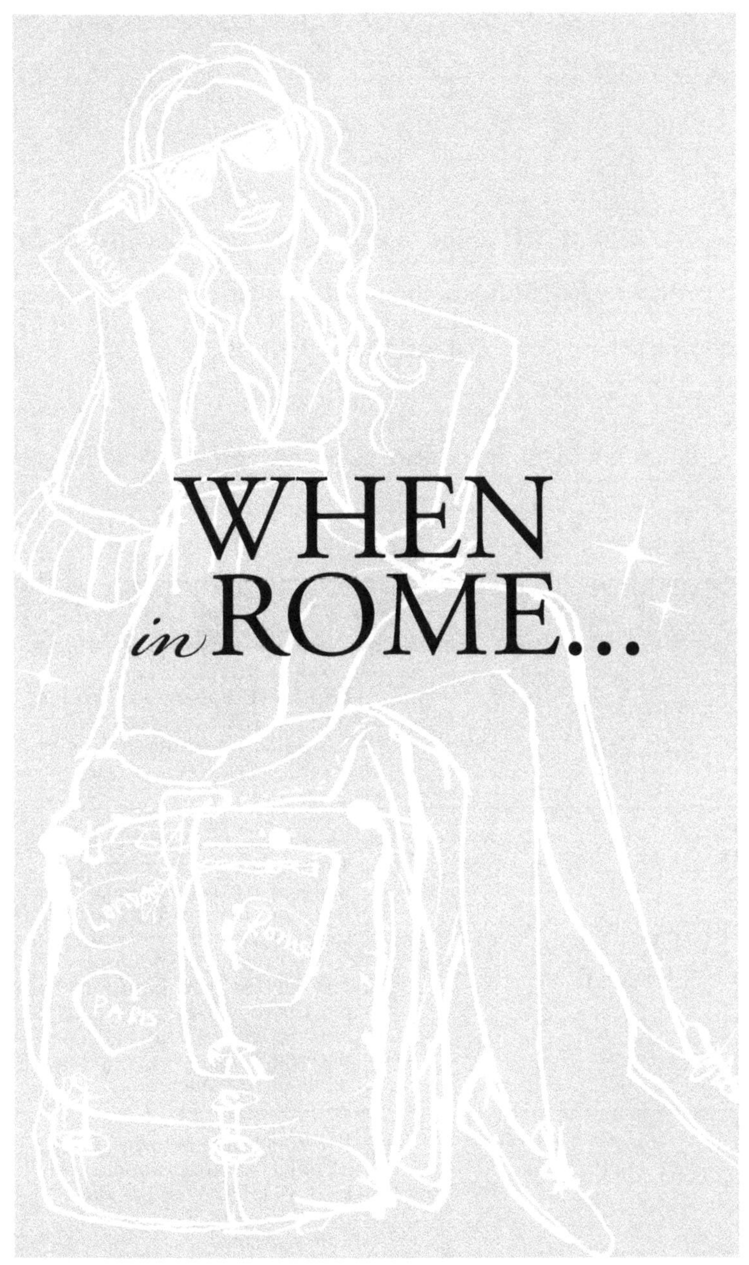

WHEN *in* ROME...

"You will do foolish things, but do them with enthusiasm."

COLETTE, FRENCH WRITER

Yes, we came to Europe to explore the sites, understand the history, see what the fuss is about Italian men, but we know deep down it's those shops that seal the deal for us.

Below is a list of my favorite places to shop. *Please* don't limit yourself to the following:

CITY	SHOP	DESCRIPTION
MYKONOS, GREECE	*Soho: Little Venice*	Expensive, gorgeous individual one-offs that you won't find in Australia. I recommend their shoes.
ISTANBUL, TURKEY	*Grand Bazzar Markets:*	Do not miss this one. Dress appropriately – the place is filled with gawking men. Buy as much as you can. It's so cheap how can you resist? Everything is fake designer, but the best part about this place is the jewelry – go crazy here; jewelry is really light, so packing it into your bakpack wont be too much of a drama.
CATANYA, SCICILY	*City, Centre*	If you get here before the rest of Italy, the prices are cheaper, so buy up! They've got most popular shops like *miss sixty* and *mango.*

ROME, ITALY	*TAD Concept store; Via del Babuno 155/a*	This is ultra cool. A lifestyle in a store. Café, music, clothes, shoes, perfume, hairstylist, homewears, furniture and even flowers. Tre chic!
FLORENCE, ITALY	*Factory Outlets*	Inquire at your hostel – everyone knows about this little gem. Just outside of Florence is a huge factory with discount designer items. Where better to grab the latest Dolce & Gabbanna for a fraction of the cost?
LONDON, ENGLAND	*Topshop*	Gorgeous mix of new trendy stuff with vintage pieces. London as we all know has great shops everywhere, but is crazy expensive, so head to places like Topshop, H&M and Zara for more reasonable fashion purchases. H&M and Zara are all over Europe, but I loved the stock in London the best. For great vintage stores head to Brick Lane; E1 6SE. This area has awesome rare gems to take back home.
	Camden Markets	Totally original items at bargain prices – come here to see what's in fashion next season.
	Portobello Markets	Portobello Road Market is one of the most famous markets in the world. It's famous for its second-hand and antique sections. Open Fridays and Saturdays.
	Beyond the Valley; London W1F 7RD	Located on Newburgh St, London. Awesome store/ gallery.

BARCELONA, SPAIN	*Loring Art; C/Gravina 8 Barcelona 08001*	Art, graphic design and fashion magazines, books and knick-knacks. Great little arty shop. Located just near Placa Catalunya.
	Street Markets, Beachside	Great little markets – pick up some cool hats, jewelry, gifts, etc.
	La Ramblas	Explore the side streets just off La Ramblas. You'll be entertained for days walking around here. The prices are reasonable and the shops are endless.
SAN SABASTIAN, SPAIN	*Beachside/Old City*	**Adolfo Dominguez** – very cool Spanish designer. **Arbelaitz** – stylish clothes and accessories in a gorgeous space. **Bonnie and Clyde & Don Pascual** – definitely worth a look.
PRAGUE, CZECH REPUBLIC	*Old City*	Prague is not on the Euro, so it's worth buying a few staples here - Jumpers, Jeans, whatever.
PARIS, FRANCE	*20th arondissement in St. Quen*	**Le Marche aux Puces**: Great Vintage pieces. Everything from Louis Vuitton to Levis.
	Ave des Champs-Elysées	Crazy prices, top designers… don't buy anything here – it'll cost half the amount of your trip. But who said anything about window shopping…one little look can't hurt…

	Montmartre	This is a great little artistic area … Take the afternoon to browse.
	Marais	Head to the back streets of this exclusive area – there are some hot little boutiques. My favorite store is called Shine; 15 rue de Poitou 75003; this has fantastic stores all around it. For one of the best vintage stores in Paris, head to **Yukiko**; 97 rue Viellie du Temple 75003. Take a credit card and prepare to fall in love.
	Galleries La Fayette; 40, Boulevard Haussmann 75009	This is mall shopping – Paris style.

Reflection on trip:

Greek Islands – Mykonos
– Santorini
– Ios

Mykonos

Turkey – Fetiq
– Instanbul

Croatia – Zagreb
– Hvar
– Dubrovnik

Italy – Bari
Napoli
Amalfi
Napoli

Sicily – Taromina
– Catanya
– Cefalu

Italy – Rome
Florence
Cinque Terra
Milan

London

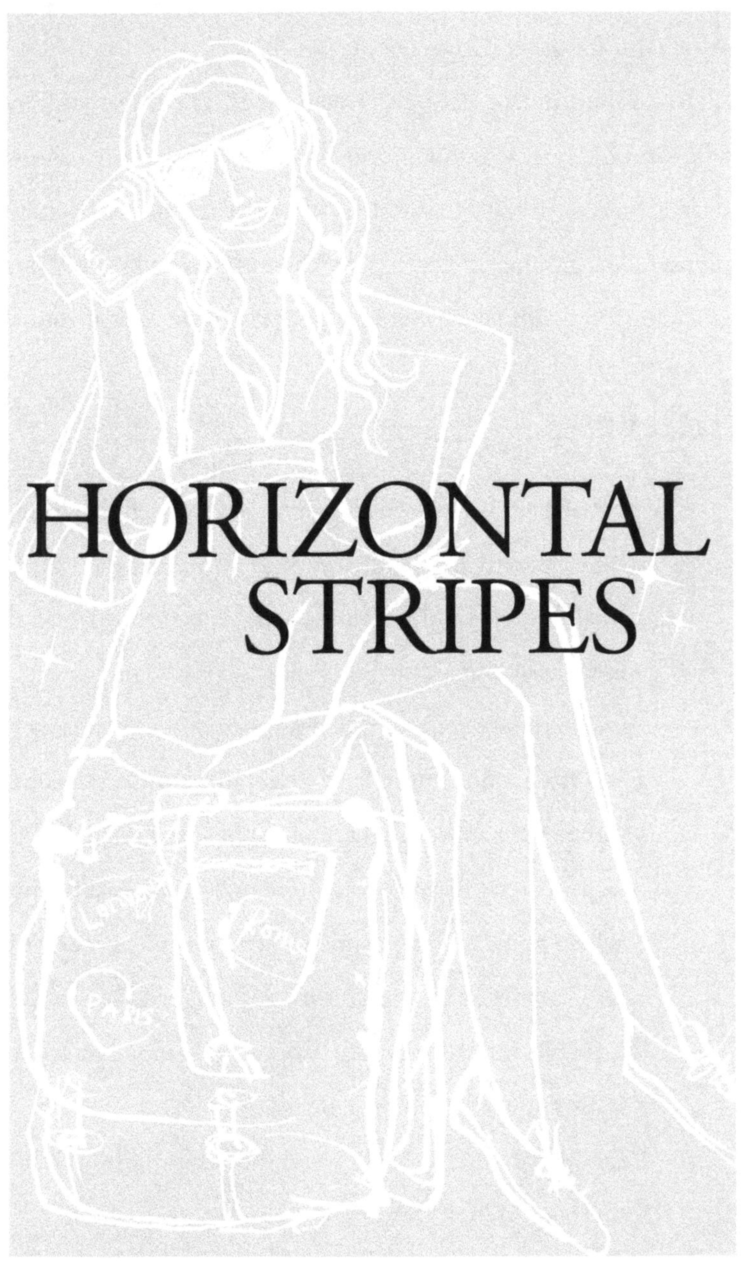

HORIZONTAL STRIPES

You wouldn't wear horizontal stripes if I paid you, right? Watch out for other dangers while travelling.

It's an unfortunate fact that women travellers need to journey with special care, especially internationally. Female concerns include sexual verbal harassment or physical assault, crude propositions, groping and even rape. These are a couple of my tips in conjunction with fellow women's tips from www.about.com:

Thieves

Thieves often perceive women as easier targets for theft than men.

- Avoid deserted streets after dark. If you can't, then carry a small, heavy flashlight in your hand. Be careful even if you have a companion.
- Some thieves prefer crowded areas. Stay alert in places such as bus stations and during street celebrations and nightclubs. I learned the hard way…don't take your Prada purse!
- Muggers aren't interested in your bra! Sew pockets into it where you can keep some money or a folded copy of your passport so that if you do get mugged, you're not left helpless. A money belt works well, too, but some thieves know about money belts.
- Leave all Tiffany's at home - rather be safe than sorry. It's something to look forward to when you come home!

 Most experts say not to resist: let your bag go and then shout for help rather than risk assault. Opening your wallet and handing over your money may be enough for the thief and you can keep your bag. If not, you'll still have most of your money in your money belt or your secret bra compartments.

Avoiding Sleazy Men

That dark Italian may be the hottest thing on the planet, but he could be looking at your bag… not your eyes. He also may want to get into your pants – it's not uncommon. Follow these tips to avoid unwanted attention:

 Consider buying a cheap wedding ring, even if you're a teenager. Especially in developing countries, a married woman is viewed as the property of another man and therefore is off limits.

 If you're being groped or touched inappropriately in a crowd, know how to say "Leave me alone!" loudly in the local language. In Spanish, for instance, learn these useful phrases:

- Salgame solo! (Leave me alone!)
- Vayase! (Go away!)
- Socorro! (Help!)
- Llama a la policia! (Call the police!)

 Carry pepper spray in case of assault and always be ready to run like the wind. If you think you're going to be raped, a surprisingly effective technique is to pretend you're going to

vomit in the man's face. Although a knee to the family jewels is sure to work, it may be grounds for arresting YOU for assault in some developing countries. If you are raped, head for your hotel or a hospital to ask for help — the police station may not be the safest place to go, depending on your location.

"Sleep with all your belongings in your sleeping bag! They can't possibly unzip your sleeping bag without waking you – and if they get as far as to your feet – KICK 'EM*!"*

SIMONE, 21

Dressing well can make a thief think you have mounds of moolah in your bag. And women's dress can be a major issue in some developing countries. Remember that until recently Afghanistan women had to cover themselves from head to toe or risk legal repercussions.

- Learn the local dress code as soon as you arrive and buy appropriate clothing locally, if necessary. In Islamic countries, lay aside your liberated notions and wear a head scarf (Hermes is already into this look in a big way!) Pack a floor-length dress with long sleeves if you're visiting places such as Iran.
- If you are going to sleep with guys overseas, make sure you do it safe. There are real diseases out there – such as AIDS, hepatitis, herpes and so on. Although they may look cute, you don't know their past. Be safe, not sorry.

Look after yourself, but don't skip the fun!

Carry a disposable camera on nights out. You don't want your expensive digital camera stolen while you're tipsy. Everyone told me to use a pouch for under my clothes, but I'm sorry, have you tried fitting such a thing in skin-tight Levis? Just be sensible and keep a watch out. I found myself becoming really alert while traveling. As soon as anyone approached me, my hand casually shot to holding my bag after a while.

Remember to Keep in Touch!

Write emails and give your family and friends a call once in a while to let them know you are alive (and make them really jealous of your amazing life).

One of the best ways to keep in touch is via SIM card. SIM cards can be bought at telephone stores or news agents.

Another good way to call home is to buy a calling card from a news agent. You can often chat for hours for a relatively small fee.

Check out http://www.overseasdigest.com/four-best-ways-to-call-home.htm for further guidelines on the best way to make calls overseas.

Bottom Line

You're a princess. You have mastered the art of confidence when entering the room at the A-list party, so don't let your talents go to waste. Look and act confident. Be alert. Be smart – common sense is your best asset and it can keep you safe.

* THIRCD
LONDON (STN) - TOURS (TUF)
Wed 17 Nov 04
Flight FR 8868
Dept STN @ 10:15am
Arrive TUF @ 12:35pm
£ 15.69

* KK Y8CE
HAHN FRANKFURT (HHN) -
LONDON STN
Tues 16th NOV 04
Flight FR 755
Dept HHN @ 14:15 Arrive STN @ 14:30

* E3G25P3
PARIS (Charles de Gaulle) → LON (LTN)
Thursday 25th NOV 04
Flight 2552
Dep 8:30am PARIS
arrive 8:45 LONDON

I WANT MORE!

I found these sites pretty useful. The more you learn from past experiences, the better your trip will be. A princess can never have too much fun!

To find out more about all my latest adventures and the most up-to-date travel advice, check out my website: **www.princesswithabackpack.com**

1. www.anytravel.com
2. www.about.com
3. www.backpackeurope.com/tips/women/
4. www.busabout.com
5. www.ciaobellatravel.com.au
6. www.christinecolumbus.com
7. www.easyjet.com
8. www.eurail.com
9. www.hihostels.com
10. www.hostelworld.com
11. www.jackiestorm.com
12. www.journeywoman.com
13. www.lonelyplanet.com
14. www.princesswithabackpack.com
15. www.ryanair.com
16. www.statravel.com.au
17. www.travellady.com
18. www.womantraveler.com
19. www.womenstravelclub.com
20. www.women-traveling.com

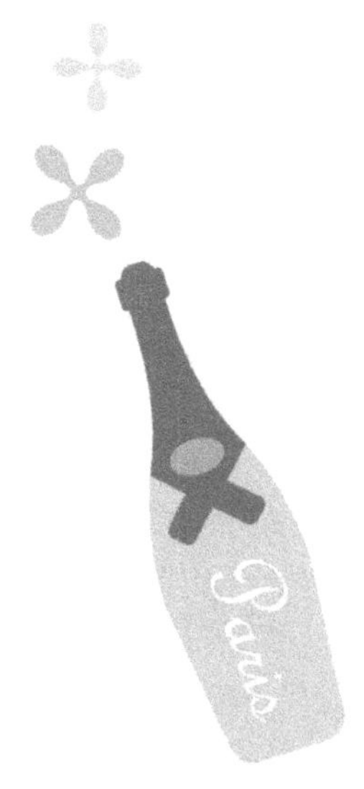

"You may be disappointed if you fail, but you are doomed if you don't try."

BEVERLY SILLS, Opera Singer

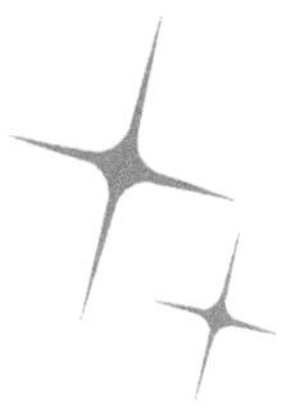

Travelling alone was something I never, ever thought I would or could do.

I am a 25-year-old female who lives in Sydney and the longest I had previously traveled solo was three days. However, when my job finished this year, I was looking to get away for a while and see the world. I did not want to drop $3,000 just to be back in Australia three weeks later; I really wanted to see the world and not do the whirlwind, blink-and-you-will-miss-it tour. All my friends were unavailable for this long journey (4 months funny that!) but it was the perfect time for me to get away, so it was either go it alone or do not go at all. The latter was just not an option.

My friends would not exactly describe me as the backpacking type, usually going for fortnightly manicures and not thinking twice about dropping $40 on dinner, didn't fit the preconceived notion I had of what a backpacker looks like.But my desire to travel outweighed my desire to stay home in my comfortable life. How do I do it though? How do I backpack but still remain, well, me throughout my travels? *Lonely Planet* is all very well and good, but it does not explain what it is like to see the world as a lone female travel and get the most out of your travels.

My sister chucked a copy of *Princess with a Backpack* with my belongings before I left and it became my bible. It has everything you need to know… from what to pack, to the best places to party and stay, this book has got it covered. I find myself flicking through it every day and think Lauren's experiences, misadventures and total chutzpah on her travels have helped me make the absolute most out of mine. I think this book will give young women the confidence to take on the world on their own and have a blast while doing so.

You don't have to twirl fire sticks and have dreadlocks to travel alone. You've just got to have the insider tips and knowledge and this book gives you just that.

"Safe travels y'all!!"

SIMONE, 25, SYDNEY, AUSTRALIA

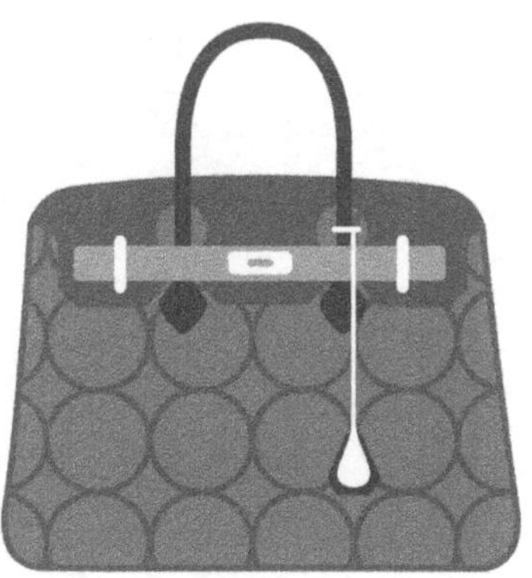